CEO
Time Matrix

BEST-CEO
Productivity Formula
Schedule Management

Applied Time Management
for

0.8% Works => 125 x Result
Corporations & Individual
Victories

A Personal Priority Construction
from
Dr. A. Riawan Amin

~ 0 ~

An On-line edition,
CEO Time Matrix
Dr. A. Riawan Amin
Cover: http://www.i-proclaim.com/project-cover-art-
preview.asp?project=A19A563B-DC8C-4A6D-B704-
1100C0FAC9E4
By I-Proclaim

1st (paperback) edition Published in Indonesia 2011
By CEO-Consult Publishing,
Jl. Kemang Utara 33, Jakarta Selatan, INDONESIA,
ceotimematrix@riawanmin.com
Copyright © 2011 by Dr. A. Riawan Amin

ISBN-13: **978-1461066064**
ISBN-10: **1461066069**

PREFACE

This essay is _significantly against_ any other 'how to' Time Management books, dedicated only for all the **geniuses** and **novices** in statesmanship. Genius is very smart people who can make improvements to bad fundamental concepts. On the contrary, novices come with fresh approach and willing to work honestly.

This essay is prohibited and extremely dangerous to people who has only **average** or **medium** skills in Time Management, because this will tell them only the truth, that might be different than many difficult less useful personal management theories, corporate affairs and leaders' activity they have learned before.

At least 6 (six) things already achieved by this book:

1 This is a nice, interesting and challenging treatise, written in plain English that is easy to be understood, by most of the people of our world. Readers can follow the data, ideas and aesthetical beauty involved.

2 This is a medium of idealism and charity. Twenty percent (20%) of its profit will be donated, to support effort to simplify world complex investment engineering works.

3 This is an integrated time management, using short and simple models to help the professional schedule.

4 This is a book of quiz and puzzles. Smart reader can enjoy them and less clever one can understand better by doing that difficult real life in the beauty of mathematics.

5 This is a book of fundamental state & leaders' managements. All ideas, tips and clues are useful.

6 This is a book of schedule engineering. All architecture techniques are packaged in geometric formats.

This book is dedicated as my gratitude to my respected parents, Mr. SM. Amin Krueng Raba Nasution and Cut Maryam Amin, and also to my parents in law, Ir. HM. Sanusi Sierad and Juanita Lendra Karaton, who taught me with the essence of my life existence and what we must do in this short life

The essence of life is on the eternity, far beyond the life itself

Let my wife Mira and three daughters Gia, Callista and Zahra, get the wisdom from this book and the life experience they collect day after day

TABLE OF CONTENTS

0008 Comprehensive Time Management Resume

DO you know *Time Management* (T-M)? The practical skill used to be taught at most management schools or courses to this day? In principle, T-M taught us how precious time is as a limited resource we all have that non-renewable in nature. What is more, if we consider the life-expectancy of average people nowadays (as of 65 to 70 years?), then we only have less than several thousand days (less by our age at present, times 365 days) left. So every year, the candles on our birthday cake should not be added in number, instead it should be taken less and less towards the final count-down eventually as we pass away. And we only have 24 hours each day (less our sleeping time), remember)? So the choice is ours: to *Use*, *Misuse* or (let others *Abuse*) our time in one way or another.

As we know, at least there are three domains of time in the life of a modern person nowadays: *personal,* and *professional* (8 hours a day). And although the T-M principles could be implemented in all, it seems that only in the professional domain it could express itself in full mode. Even in this domain, especially for those who work for a company or in an organization setting, there are differences in T-M application according to the kind and level of jobs involved. T-M for "blue-collar" workers, for instance, is certainly different than that for their "white-collars" fellows. So is with; supervisors, managers, directors and up to the *Chief Executive Officers* (CEO).

Even though it seems similar to other professions (such as: entrepreneurs, freelance workers and that of artists), this article is dedicated primarily to CEO, (and those who aspire to be one), who are sitting in the peak of organizational pyramids. They, who generally have significant powers, responsibilities and supporting facilities compared to most others. As such, the CEOs could actually implement the T-M to the fullest, and make themselves much more productive – if they so desire. And should they wish to spend the additional time 'created' or saved to enrich their personal, social (and that of spiritual to be completed) life-spheres then, it is also up to them.

Efficient-Effective & Urgent-Important

The pair of terms just firstly mentioned, *efficiency* (do in less time) and *effectiveness* (which produced results) are the most often used concepts in varied Time Management theories. Although the day of the old-fashioned "efficiency expert" is long gone, today's management thinks in terms of effectiveness, which is a broader and more useful concept. Efficiency, as we know, concerns about the best way of doing an assigned task. Effectiveness and industry's less cost, on the other hand, concerns *the best use of time* in achieving the objective– which may or may not include doing the particular task in question at all. Sound management involves thinking of effectiveness first and efficiency second. In other words, doing things right beautifully is not as important as doing the right things adequately.

On the other hand, there is another pair of terms often used in T-M: *Urgent* and *Important*. Both are popularly explained in a matrix form. It consists of: Important-and-Urgent, Important-but-not-Urgent, Urgent-but-not-Important and Not-Urgent-and-Not-Important quadrants. Of course, as the theory suggests, we all have to focus our energy in doing the tasks which mainly belong to the second (*Important-but-not-Urgent*) quadrant, in order to be effective. Using the same approach, this article will explain another concept of Time-Matrix – primarily dedicated to the CEO of modern days.

The Pareto Principle

Still regarding effectiveness and productivity, there was an Italian early nineteen-century economist, Wilfredo Pareto who observed that 20 percent of the British people owned 80 percent of his country's accumulated wealth. It was the official start of a then becomes famous rule now known as the Pareto principle, or the 80/20 rules that, surprisingly enough; also apply to many areas of human activity. For example, it could be said that 80 percent of our productivity and achievements comes from 20 percent of our day, 80% of our revenue will come from 20% of our clients and so on. In other words, a small part of what we do, will contribute the most to our overall results, if only we focus to that vital-few "to-be-done" tasks and skip the trivial-many "to-be-neglected" activities. Based on this rule, a CEO could 'created' or save much more time - professionally speaking.

Trying to apply these considerations into a CEO work context, has inspired me a new Time Management approach that I named *"CEO Time Matrix"* which I would like to explain hereby (see diagram below).

THE CEO Time Matrix

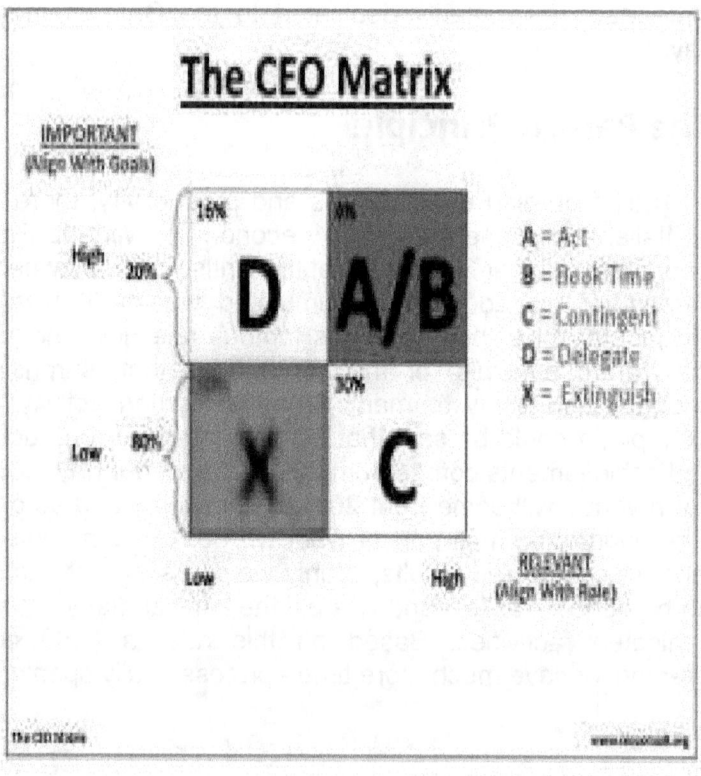

It consists of 4 time-allocated quadrants: A/B (*Act now/Booked time*), C (*Contingent*), D (*Delegate*) and X for *eXtinguish* – each explained as follow:

A (Act now!) = Things we have to act right now, immediately and not to be delayed.

B (Booked time!) = Things we plan to do soon or in the near future. Actually, these may or may not be acted upon by us eventually, but at least they are listed as our booked "To Do List". The **A/B** then represent a choice between each: DO it now or Do it later (as planned).

C (Contingent or Contingency) = As the term implies, it means things to be spared of. Do when the need arise – just in case. It is better to have a contingency in place, but does not need to do it then, than the other way around.

D (Delegate) = Either to our dedicated staffs or be outsourced to specially hired outsiders; but not to be done by ourselves. Just consider which is more important: Doing the task ourselves or getting the task Done (by involving others)?

X (eXtinguish) = Things to be eliminated. To do without at all. As for the methods in this regards, there are ways to do so as well as many "time wasters" to be avoided by any CEO – such as many: Information overload, Junk mails (including e-mails), Interruptions, Meetings, etc. .

IMPORTANT & RELEVANT = Unlike a classic differentiation between the Urgent and Important matters, the CEO Time Matrix divides all incoming "To-Do" stimuli into the Important (aligned with Goal) and Relevant (aligned with Role) ones. Each has its own *High* and *Low* quadrants.

GOAL = Valuable cleared things we choose to be accomplished. It may be for a Short, Medium or Long term ones – both tangible and intangible. It may be Personal, Team or Organizational in nature – the accomplishment of which will measure and determine our success in life. So everything that aligned with our Goal is the *important* matters for us. Regarding goal, perhaps it is inspiring to note the following pray of St. Francis: "*God, give me the serenity to accept the things I cannot change, the courage to change the things I can and the Wisdom to know the difference*".

ROLE = A position we hold among others with all the Rights and Responsibilities involved. It may be determined by *Birth* (a family tree, for instance) or that of *Choices* such as a career path we pursue (as CEO). And everything that aligned with our Role is the *Relevant* matters.

Implementation of CEO Time Matrix:

To implement the CEO Matrix, first of all we should apply the Pareto's 80/20 rule by extinguish all "Not-to-be-Done" tasks by 64% in the **X** quadrant (since they belong to the Low-Low category in both Importance and Relevancy), 30% Contingency for the **C** quadrant (may not be done anyway). And from the rest 20% "To-be-Done" tasks, we apply the 80/20 rule again, so we have 16% to be Delegated to others (belong to **D** quadrant) and only the rest 4% "Act Now/Book time Later" we should do ourselves (for **A/B** quadrant) which have a High-High category to be prioritized. Noting the 96% time left, we can imagine how much times could potentially be added or saved, if this Time Matrix has been practiced consistently, don't you agree?

Of course, in real life situations, the application of CEO Time Matrix will depend on each individual values and concerns. Its function is more of a framework to simplify things in order to manage our precious time effectively. It is estimated that, a CEO, could produce 25 times more results by implementing this new Time Management approach. Hopefully this new thought will provide significant benefits to all of us. Good luck and have a good time!

Dr. A. Riawan Amin. is the former CEO of the most profitable Islamic bank (Bank Muamalat Indonesia, 1999 – 2009), and the President of Indonesian Islamic Bank Association (ASBISINDO). He is also a writer of bestselling books *Celestial Management, Satanic Finance & You are (not) the boss*, and now become a sought-after speaker – local and abroad.

0016. INTRODUCTION:
Non Renewable Essence of Time & Management

*To everything there is a season, and a time to every purpose
under heaven: A time to be born, and a time to die; a time to
plant, and a time to pluck up that which is planted; A time to
kill, and a time to heal; a time to break down, and a time to
build up;[1]*

Time, whether you like it or not, is essential as a non
renewable resource. It is the necessary ingredient of life, but
should be managed very-very well, because no addition could
be given to it. So then, please use it very carefully.[2] The
higher your position in organization, and the more people you
lead, the more important this book could help you.

On the other hand, the management plans, do, act and re-
check their activities within the time. The higher the
management, the more important they do, more responsibility
and consequences involved.

Please do not let this book unread, because it contains so
many useful tips and ideas that may change and improve your
life significantly.

---

[1] *A Time for Everything.* by Matt Slick. "There is an appointed time for
everything. And there is a time for every event under heaven;
http://www.fleurdelis.com/toeverythingthereisaseason.htm;

[2] *Time management* is the act or process of exercising conscious control
over the amount of time spent on specific activities, especially to increase
efficiency;
http://www.en.wikipedia.org/wiki/**Time_management***;*

0017.   The 12500% Result!? How to make it Possible?

Would you please imagine what could you be if were given 124 professional lives more? Sure, you can do many things by your 125 times capacity, both for your professional, personal and spiritual life as well. You can be a better person!

The 125 times or 12500% capacity means that you could do more than 50% of your result by working 100% /125= 0.8% or your time. Is that possible? Really?

Yes, you could do that if you carefully examining the comparison of result quantities against the time spent to get it done. So then you could select the activities that could give you good output vs input ratio.[3]

If you really work only on activities of high output in put ratio, then you are a more efficient person! If those things gives better and more relevant impact, then you also a very effective in your personal role in life.[4]

Sure, to be a better person, you must arrange your life and time schedule smarter to gain more extra time budget!

---

[3] Usually this *ratio* is in the form of an average, expressing the total *output* divided by the total *input*. Productivity is a measure of *output* from a production process; http://www.en.wikipedia.org/wiki/Productivity

[4] Lon Roberts (1994: 19): efficiency: "to the degree of economy with which the process consumes resources-especially time and money," while effectiveness is "how well the process actually accomplishes its intended purpose, here again from the customer's point of view."; http://www.enotes.com/management-encyclopedia/effectiveness-efficiency

0018. Additional Time! Gaining More on Priority Items

Since people could rarely change their absolute time schedule, they use the productivity to measure effectiveness and multiplication of capacity of the useful activity done.[5]

This book is a breaker to shock your intellectual attitudes. Do you use your time usefully? Only working on things that bringing significant impacts? Are you sure?

Whether you had use your time efficiently, or just wasting your time for trivial works, both your remaining time for chances are limited. So, use it wise-fully!

Let us make the most effective and the most efficient of your remaining time exist. Let us start it now and make successes starting from the near future.

In other words: "goal setting". Please re-think about your desired objectives and the remaining time to get it done. Whether for good or bad, you must get the best of your in the meaningful area of your wildest dream ever.[6]

---

[5] The ancient Greeks had two words for time, chronos and kairos. While the former refers to chronological or sequential time, the latter signifies a time in between, a moment of indeterminate time in which something special happens. What the special something is depends on who is using the word. While chronos is quantitative, kairos has a qualitative nature. http://www.en.wikipedia.org/wiki/Kairos;

[6] We set ourselves clear **goals** that can achieve. Feedback helps. Directional **goals** narrow our thinking. Accuracy **goals** keep us thinking and more focused on. http://www.changingminds.org › Explanations › Theories

0019. Additional Works! Achieving on More New Fields

Supposing that you could get more than 50% of your important objectives by doing only 0.8% of your time, and then you are having a lot of more flexibility.

If you just want to achieve slightly above 100% of your objectives, then you could work best for 2 x 0.8% = 1.6% of your time budget. Is it interesting? Getting more than 100% result by using only 1.6% of your time? Fantastic!

However, if you are not a lazy person, then you could utilize 100% - 1.6% = 98.4% of your gained extra time for doing more useful things as you would like!

Even though diligent and industrious person mostly perceived better than lazy one, the smart person does not have to work all the time. They also need to be rejuvenated.

It needs a balance between production and capacity advancement. Too much production will reduce capacity improvement, while too much capability improvement shall not produce much. Do production, but increase the capacity.[7]

There is an old story of three carpenters. The one is industrious but forget to sharpen the axe. The second is sharpening the axe, but not cutting trees, the third wins them all because do the production and capacity building as well.

---

[7] Stephen R. **Covey**, _The Seven Habits of Highly Effective People_: (Production versus building **Production Capacity**) balance for interdependence.   http://www.build-creative-writing-ideas.com/stephen-covey.html

0020. Additional Choice! Enjoying More Life Flexibility

It is clear that you could have more flexibility, if could gain more than 100% results by 1.6% works. You would plan the remaining 98.4% time for any other purposes on your favor. Now you could control your life much better.

You must have options in order to get a happy life. If it is only one possibility and no other option exist, then you are in forced life's destiny and could not change your fate.[8]

Having options mean that you could choose better alternatives by yourself. Even though both are awful, you still have a freedom to choose the better of possibilities.

Back to the remaining 98.4% time rest, you could do in between of 12400% more productions and 12400% more capacity advancement. The correct number is yours, if and only if you have the freedom to choose.[9]

So, finally whoever you are, whether a diligent or the lazy one: Better time management will always be better to provide you a lot of options, to make the best of your life.

---

[8] What is the significance of **fatalism**? **Fatalism** is a belief that events are determined by fate. **Fatalism** is a belief that we have to accept the outcome of events.
http://www.angelfire.com/md2/timewarp/**fatalism**.html

[9] **Maximax** strategy maximizes the **maximum** gain. The **maximin** criterion suggests that the decision-maker should choose the alternative which maximises the minimum payoff.
http://www.doc.ic.ac.uk/~frk/frank/da/1.%20decision%20analysis%20intr o.pdf

0021. Constructing More Sense on Time Management

Clock-wise sharp time management, especially in German style could be very frightening. People must act sharply punctual 'korekt' to be as perfect as possible. They produce more machines and large technological works.[10]

On the contrary, life could be very flexible. Next country adjacent to them break all of their rules, but also very successful. They enjoy their life in arts and beauties; have lots of free time, but still gaining much money in aesthetics.

Could you guess which one is the lazy country adjacent to German? What? Yes, it is France! The lazy French people making beautiful products from small cheap raw materials. They sold lipstick, mascara, powder, fragrance, wine bags and beauty everywhere.

Sure, you were not German or French, so you could choose the proper style between the two according to your comfort and resources possible. You have the right to win.

Who ever you are and how dark you're past life, will not dirt your future. Your next day still be as white as a clean paper. Only you yourself have the right to draw on it. It is now, or never. The decision is yours.[11]

---

[10] **German metalworks**. BERLIN, With a recession looming in Europe's biggest economy, "Germany's largest industrial trade union IG Metall"; http://www.archives.dawn.com/2008/11/01/ebr11.htm:

[11] **To be, or not to be**" is the opening line of a monologue from William Shakespeare's play Hamlet (written about 1600), act three, scene one. It is the best-known. http://www.en.wikipedia.org/wiki/To_be,_or_not_to_be:

0022. **CHAPTER-I:**
Advancement of Pareto's 80/20 Statistics

Rule 80/20 had been famously known as Pareto's Law. Although 100% results are from 100% resources, most of empirical evidences proven that 80% results come from only 20% resources (20% works, 20% workers, 20% time, 20% budget and many others).[12]

Off course, the numbers were not sharply 80/20, but they are true and easy to be remembered. Utilizing this statistical law could make significant changes to your achievement. It does increase your effectiveness!

Advance application of Pareto's statistic for two variables is (80/20) (80/20), means that the result is 80% x 80% = 64% from 20% x 20% = 4% works.

For three variables application, the Pareto's statistic for minimum work needed is 20% x 20% x 20% = 0.8%, but it brings result of 80% x 80% x 80% = 53.2%. Wonderful!

It implies that by employing just 0.8% resources, you could get 53.2% of the result. It is even magical compared to the common people's 50:50 or 50% chances to win.[13]

---

[12] **Pareto's** Principle or the **80-20** Rule helps you manage those things that really make a difference to your results.
http://www.management.about.com/cs/generalmanagement/a/**Pareto**0812 02.htm;

[13] Presents some of the most common 50-50 choices that arise. Lets see if the 50-50-90 rule applies to you if you have a **50-50 chance;**
http://www.funtrivia.com/trivia-quiz;

0023. The Normal Distribution and Pareto's Simplicity

Wilfredo Pareto had simplified the common statistical "Normal Distribution" curve that shows those facts. All of the result possibilities are normally lies around its average. The closer to the average, the more possibility occurs. So its graph is plot like a "bell-shape", most close to its average.[14]

Since almost all of the data possible are surrounding but not exactly equal to its average (they have own deviations), then there is a "Standard Deviation" as least squares weighted average of all data deviation possible.[15]

The amount of possibilities among its average, one Standard Deviation less to one Standard Deviation more is approximately 68%. Possibilities among its average, two Standard Deviation less to two Standard Deviation more is approximately 95%.

So then Pareto's law is possibilities among its average, one and a half Standard Deviation less to one and Standard Deviation more is approximately 83.5%. Then 80% is a better number for much more memorable purpose. It is very smart and simple easy to memorize truth. Bravo!

---

[14] The **normal distributions** are a very important class of statistical distributions. All **normal distributions** are symmetric and have bell-shaped. http://www-stat.stanford.edu/~naras/

[15] **Standard deviation** is a widely used measurement of variability or diversity used in statistics and probability theory. It shows how much variation or "dispersion". http://www.en.wikipedia.org/wiki/Standard_deviation

0024. Common Pareto's 80/20 Application for Leaders

Since CEO (it sounds Italian like Pareto, but stand for English abbreviation for Chief Executive Officer) deals with many things, the logic of significance in "Normal Distribution" as simplified by Wilfredo Pareto becomes very important. It does help in most of the decision making.[16]

First, as a very important person the CEO is very much responsible for important matters. He or she must not do trivial things that could be avoided or delegated to subordinates. The CEO must also select disturbances or problems those are not relevant to the company.

Second, as a head of organization the CEO must work thru chain of commands. He or she must let the proper organizational function doing their job. The CEO must also select the job that relevant to his organizational position.

Wow, very common sense and logical! Do they understand those principles? Yes, but do they really do those? Not always. Why? Because CEO normally thinks that they are free to do most favorable things, because they are the boss of all people in the organization! It is a position power!

Wrong! The position must be related to CEO's role and function because it is a duty, an assignment, not just an amusement for the personal ego and preferences of the CEO. Organization needs leaders who work their role very well!

---

[16] A **CEO's responsibilities**: everything, especially in a startup. The CEO is responsible for the success or failure of the company. Operations, marketing, strategy. http://www.steverrobbins.com/articles/ceojob

0025. Importance as the Life and Professional Priority

Almost every person and CEO knows very well that they must prioritize their resources on important results, but what is the meaning important? What this definition of importance impacting the organization? Sure, they must bring it to the conscious level to perform well.[17]

In short, important are things significantly impacting the whole. It is a continuum from the moderately important (average) in the middle to the most important on the very right and the least important on its very leftmost.

This dichotomy approach helps the people to define things according to importance. Higher than average is definitely important and lower than average is not so important. All jobs could be properly placed in this line.

When it comes to an organization, the importance then should be reviewed according to the organizational standard. It is a collective one, more than any personal interest of its member or the CEO's self preferences.

People should submit their personal interest, under the common objective of the organization.[18]

---

[17] Strongly affecting the course of events or the nature of things; significant: (i.e. **important** message that must get through; close friends whose **important** to me). http://www.thefreedictionary.com/**important**;

[18] Definition of **organization**: A social unit of people, systematically structured and managed to meet a need or to pursue collective goals on a continuing basis. http://www.businessdictionary.com/definition/**organization**.html.

0026. Relevance as the Personal Role on the System

Relevance is appropriateness to the organizational role and function. Even if the general is a better sniper than the assigned soldier, it is improper to do the sniper jobs solely by himself (or herself). Why, because the role is to lead and not to let the subordinates work alone.[19]

That is just a beautiful concept. It does not always done, because not all CEOs really want to perform in its role. If the positions seen more as a reward rather than a duty, the granted persons will do things that they loved most. Natural!

At the relevance continuum, the right ride of the average is highly relevant matters and on its left are not so (or less) relevant roles. According to "Normal Distribution" and Pareto statistics, most of the probabilities lies close to its average, so then this below vs above average is useful.

Let us also discuss the term "urgency" here, since it appears most. Is it related more to the role or to CEO's personal preference? The CEO job itself is for a high level strategic and long range. No urgency possibility should occur at the organizational CEO levels![20]

---

[19] Typically, the **CEO** has responsibilities as a communicator, decision maker, leader, and manager. The communicator **role** can involve the press and the rest of society; http://www.en.wikipedia.org/wiki/Chief_executive_officer;

[20] **Urgency** is the quality or condition of being urgent, needing quick attention. **Urgency** may also refer to: Pan-pan, international radio call for an emergency posing; http://www.en.wikipedia.org/wiki/**Urgency**;

0027. The Importance vs Relevance Scale Quadrants

Those two continuums of Importance and Relevance could be combined and easily understood at Cartesian XY plane. Its absis (horizontal X-axis) is the Importance and Relevance as its ordinate (vertical Y-axis).[21]

First, because the CEO and all member of the organization must make their decision based on the organizational importance. The sacred mission then segregated on the organizational chain of command and functional roles relevant to generally assigned functions.

Second, because the CEO and all functions of the organization is just a structural adaptation to perform the institutional importance. The sacred mission of the organizational importance could not be adjusted to non purposive assigned functions of the organization.

Is it a big difference if we use relevance as horizontal-axis and importance as vertical-axis? Better not doing that. Graphically, the X could be Vertical and Y can be horizontal, but Importance is more logical to be the horizontal and relevance be its vertical-axis; at least psychologically.[22]

---

[21] A plane with x and y-axes defined is often referred to as the **Cartesian** plane or **xy** plane. The value of x is called the x-coordinate or abscissa and the value of y is called the y-coordinate or ordinate. http://www.en.wikipedia.org/wiki/**Cartesian**_coordinate_system;

[22] Decide which variable will be plotted on the **horizontal axis**. Put the suspected **cause** on the **horizontal axis** if showing a **cause effect** relationship. Draw and label. http://www.slideshare.net/centenvir/rkfl-problem-solving;

0028. 1st Section: Low Importance + Low Relevance

Please start on the South-west side of our Importance vs Relevance's Cartesian plane. Left means that they are less or low Importance as the base for decision making. Lower than average Relevance means that they mostly not suitable to be done by the CEO. But it could be very much tempting:

1)This case might comes earlier than others
2)CEO's taste might favor this job more than others
3)They could be need to be solved quicker than others
4)Only small amount of time and budget needed
5)The subordinate might proposed to solve them now
6)Share holder could instruct CEO to solve it quickly
7)Public pressure needs CEO to decide democratically

Sincerely those thing could not be pushed to be Important nor Relevant for the CEO position. Urgency will not be a relevant issue for CEO decisions. But surprisingly there are too many CEOs still working on urgent matters regardless of its Importance neither its Relevance.

Please consider that CEO has better helicopter view of the organizational problems than any others. Please be calm and still independent on decision making. Remember the story of 5 blind and an elephant? Democratic decision making will not help much in these cases.[23]

---

[23] It was six men of Indostan To learning much inclined, Who went to see the **Elephant** (Though five of them were **blind**), That each by observation. Does voting helps here? http://www.en.wikisource.org/wiki/ .../The_Blind_Men_and_the_Elephant

0029. 2nd Section: High Importance, but Low Relevance

Let us examine the South-east side of our Importance vs Relevance's Cartesian plane. Right means that they are very or high Importance as the base for decision making. Lower than average Relevance means that they mostly not suitable to be done by the CEO. But it could involve strong influence:

1) This case is acclaimed as very important by all
2) CEO act might be expected very hard on this job
3) They could be need to be solved quicker than others
4) Very big amount of time and budget involved here
5) Subordinate are not confident solve it by themselves
6) Share holder could instruct CEO to solve it directly
7) Public pressure needs CEO to decide it personally

Sincerely that thing is actually Important but not Relevant for the CEO position. Personal appearance will not be a relevant issue for CEO decisions. But surprisingly there are too many CEOs still working on Important matters regardless of its Relevance to the CEO's role.

Please consider that CEO does not have to work on Important problem by themselves. Please be calm and still highly rational on decision making, then let subordinate do it. What makes Napoleon Bonaparte fail? Too much handling trivial cases by his own.[24]

---

[24] Sometimes there are tasks in an office that are important but are also good if done by trusted delegated person.
http://www.articles.directorym.com/**Delegating_Office_Tasks_Napoleon_OH-r1**

0030. 3nd Section: Low Importance, but High Relevance

Now we go to the North-west side of our Importance vs Relevance's Cartesian plane. Left means that they are less or low Importance as the base for decision making. Higher than average Relevance means that they are suitably be done by the CEO. But it could be very much disturbing:

1)This case might asked to be done by subordinates
2)CEO's taste might dislike this job more than others
3)We could be never be sure if it should really occur
4)Long span of risky time and budget consequences
5)It contains legal documents and complex settings
6)Share holder might worried if this rare case appear
7)Public pressure needs CEO to be extremely perfect

Sincerely those things are not really Important but very much Relevant for the CEO position. Fail to survive it could be very bitter CEO positions. But surprisingly there are too many CEOs still delegating this sensitive matter to subordinate regardless of its Relevance for CEO position.

Please consider that CEO in the Key Stone of the arch of organizational structures and must be extremely strong in its passive function. Please be diligent and keep systematic filing on important documents. Remember the heavy function of the passive key stone in an arch? It means everything![25]

---

[25] The **keystone** is the most important stone in an **arch** bridge, without this stone the **arch** would collapse. The **keystone** holds the **arch** together. http://www.technologystudent.com/struct1/**arch**1.htm

0031. 4th Section: High Importance + High Relevance

Let us examine the North-east side of our Importance vs Relevance's Cartesian plane. Right means that they are very or high Importance as the base for decision making. Higher than average Relevance means that they mostly very suitable to be done by the CEO. But it could some times not handle as proper:

> 1)This is thought as could be done by subordinates
> 2)CEO act might be perceived as not yet necessary
> 3)They need to be solved but it is very unpleasant
> 4)They need just small amount of time and budget
> 5)The CEOs are not confident solve it by themselves
> 6)Share holder could advise CEO not to solve it now
> 7)All members need CEO to decide it democratically

Since these things are basically Important and Relevant for the CEO position, individual favor will not be a relevant issue for CEO decisions. But surprisingly there are too many CEOs still delegating this Important function regardless of its Relevance to the trusted subordinates.

Please consider that CEO must work on Important and relevant troubles by themselves. Please be calm and still be sensitive on handling these, please let no subordinate does it. What makes Toyotomi Shogunate disappear? Too much delegating Important and Relevant matters to Tokugawa.²⁶

---

²⁶ **Hideyoshi** believed that his vassals would be loyal to his heir. He had a lot of **trust** in his great friend, Tokugawa **Ieyasu**. However, he was wrong to **trust** him. http://www.esl.fis.edu/learners/support/hum/text/wh465.htm

0032. 5th Sub: Importance+Relevance, Not Urgent

The Pareto 80/20 law will be very essential in urgency matters of the North-east corner (High Importance + High Relevance). Now things are clear. It must be done by the CEO and no others could do it better for the seek of the organization. It is now just the game of buying time.

Please check and re-check it again carefully. Do they have to be done at the same time. Must it be done now or at the near future? Only few of them!

Most of them (approximately 80% as Pareto said), could be done later. Some even have to be done later, since they cannot be done now for some reasons. They do mean that CEO has more time for doing strategic jobs perfectly.

What must we do? File them on the tickler system based on their due dated, but please giving ample time to do them as proper before their due date.[27]

The most essential thing here is make the filing based on their due reviewed dates, not on their starting date of existence, because these is an active filing system, different than contingency passive document filing we've done before!

---

[27] A TICKLER system is a dated filing system that eliminates the piles, files and lists that clutter up your life. The system consists of 43 folders: one for each month, labeled January-December and one for each day of the month, labeled 1-31. http://www.overhall.com/tickler_file.htm;

0033.   6th Sub Section: Importance+Relevance, Urgent!

Like the "My Way" song,[28] now the end is near, after all. This is very significant the end of the thousands of your job possibilities. These Important works must be done by the Relevance of CEO role on very urgent schedules. Finally!

The final curtain here, as successfully ticklered and reviewed, now must be done by the CEOs themselves. Please do your best, because this is the proper time to do them. No other schedule is more suitable for doing that later.

Also check some key measures relevant to be success in that job:
1)Never forget to use your common sense, always!
2)Make sure that you have adequate resources for it
3)Kill the problem first, never let them appear again
4)Solve only them, after you could not prevent them
5)Understand its totality before making part analysis
6)Smile is a great help, a nice charity to your heart
7)Be independent: hear others, but only do your own
8)Be decisive, make timely decision when needed
9)Never delay or postpone these, they will come again

Please be Positive, Restrain and Concern. Do these all bold and consciously as planned. Please wisely think about the future impact of your CEO strategic decision making.

---

[28] **"My Way"** is a **song** popularized by Frank Sinatra. Its lyrics were written by Paul Anka and set to **music** based on the French **song** "Comme d'habitude" composed.
http://www.en.wikipedia.org/wiki/My_Way_(song)

CEO Time-Matrix

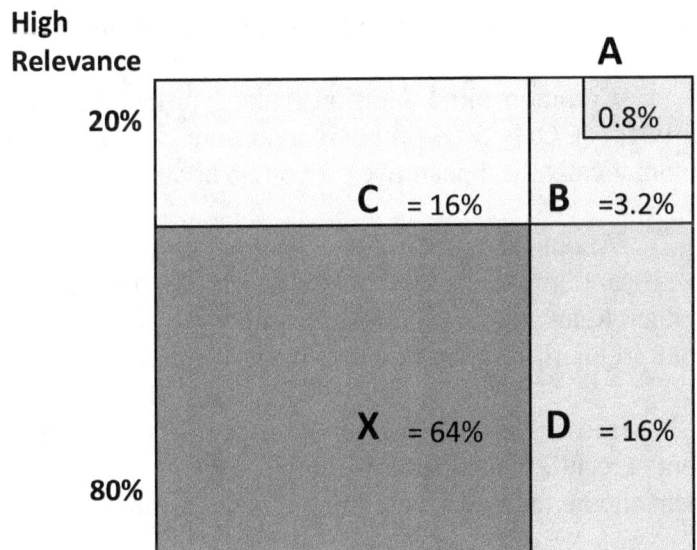

X= 80% x 80% = 64%
D= 20% x 80% = 16%
C= 80% x 20% = 16%
(A+B)= 20% x 20% = 4%
B= 80% x 20% x 20% = 3.2%
A= 20% x 20% x 20% = 0.8%

0035. **CHAPTER-II:**

The X (cross), or Extinguish Quadrant (64% Less)

Interesting thing will happen if your problem only 36% from the total. It means that you drop (cross) or extinguish 64% of all your problems. Just try to cross (X) them. Let us call this case as X (crossed-out) quadrant.

Common blind decision making probability is 50:50 (fifty-fifty). Only 50% problem is relevant. The 50% rest will automatically disappear, even if you do nothing on them.

About 50%-64% of the total problem give no significant impact to the organization (not Important) and neither Relevant to your role. In other words: they are not your problem. They belong to somebody else.[29]

Please do not work on other people's problem, since yours are still many. Time is limited. Cross (X) or extinguish them and be focused on the Important+Relevants only.[30]

CEO must focus on the work to lead the organization, so please D (delegate) as many job as possible to Able and Willing subordinates to make organization works.

---

[29] *Irrelevant problem* identified in main question. No scientific research is possible on the basis of the problem that you have identified in the main question. http://www.let.ru.nl/worldwidewriting/English/

[30] Having discussed the topic of obsession, here I'd like to go back to the topic of *focus*. *Focus* is essential to achieve anything we want in *life*. http://www. www.lifeoptimizer.org/.../how-to-**focus**-five-levels-of-mental-**focus**

0036. Deleting All Low Importance + Low Relevance

Please make sure that the problem you Extinguish (X) are not Important and neither Relevant to you. Not solving them gives no bad consequences to your role and mission. So, why should investing your time there. You better leave them.

Many people want to Extinguish (X-cross) their problem, but still do not know which of them could easily be thrown at no negative consequences. They are that gives no significant impact and not suitable for your position.

If you were the CEO, this bold and decisive decision becomes more strategic. The CEO must quickly identify and Extinguish (X-cross) the Unimportant and irrelevant ones.[31]

How if the Importance and Relevance did not clearly seen at the problems? If you are not sure about them, then they should be Extinguished (X-cross) now. Drop them now.

What happen if the Importance and Relevance of those problems later be known as very high? Those will be the case for next time. Extinguished (X-cross) now. There is nothing to be worried except the fear itself.[32]

---

[31] For *CEOs*, creativity is now the most *important* leadership quality for success in business, outweighing even integrity and global thinking, http://www.fastcompany.com/.../creativity-the-most-**important-**leadership

[32] The quote by Roosevelt, "*There is nothing* to fear but *fear itself,*" place of knowing and living that *there* is really *nothing* to fear *except fear itself.* http://www.innerworkspublishing.com/news/vol3/awareness2.htm

0037. Save 80% x 80% = 64% of Potential Time Waster

Using the Pareto's 80/20 statistical truth (conceptual and empirical), you must Extinguish (X-cross) 80% activities that bring only 20% results. For dual activities, the number is 80% x 80% = 64%, such a simple big number to find.

By Extinguishing (X-cross) them, you could get 64% time saving by not doing trivial many. At least you could enjoy the miracle now, but the magic will still continue.[33]

Strategic understanding on what things which do not belong to you, shall make your CEO works more effective. You do not have to work on less Important and less Relevant matters any longer. You are free, starts from today.

This also gives you ammunition to do more magic and makes your performance even better. Pareto and other statistical are excellent concept, but it needs smartness and creativity to properly employ them in real life.

Multiplying the CEO capacity is no longer a dream. It is proven as possible and works in many places world-wide.[34]

---

[33] Articles that demonstrate the *pareto* principle in practice through real life and business examples and teach you how to apply the *pareto* principle in your own life. http://www.shmula.com/category/**pareto-principle**

[34] The 10x *CEO* - a place where exceptional *CEOs* meet and learn new insights and collaborate in a high level community of exceptional *CEO* and COOs. http://www.ceoproject.org

0038. Only 36% Remaining, be 267% Bigger in Capacity

By Extinguishing (X-cross) 80% x 80% = 64% time waster, you still have to work on 100% - 64%= 36% rest. Your loss because of the 64% decreasing is just 20% x 20% = 4%. Then you had gaining 64% of the total time by sacrificing only 4% of your performance. Then you still hold the 100% -4% = 96% of the starting performance. You are in the right track to become a highly competitive CEO ever.

If you then reinvesting the total of 64% CEO time addition found, new wonderful things might happen. It could be 96% x (100% /36%) = 267%. So, you get 267% -100% = 167% additional CEO performances. Wonderful![35]

Now you already enjoy 100% of your second life and 67% of your third life, while you are still alive! Fantastic!

What next? You could celebrate and enjoy it, but your magic could still be uplifted to a better productivity level.

Sure, that you can read that in the next chapter of this book, but the most important now is to take a deep breath. Take an ample rest, since you had travelled almost three times of your standard living (at least mentally).

Rejuvenation, mental rest and preparation for the next creation are simply called as "recreation". It does mean really a "re-creation", while you are now created as a new person!

---

[35] *Productivity* is a measure of the efficiency of production. *Productivity* is a ratio of what is produced to what is required to produce it. Usually this ratio is the form. http://www.en.wikipedia.org/wiki/**Productivity**

0039. Enjoy 167% Extra Time for More Opportunities

Applying the SWOT[36] (strengths, weaknesses, opportunities and threats) strategic assessment, now you are 167% ready for the greater responsibility and performances.

Extinguishing 80% x 80% = 64% of your time waster, means that you have already run away from the place of so many Threats hitting on your Weaknesses (must avoided WT quadrant). You had already freed from failure possibilities.

Off course you still have the remaining Threats on your Strengths and some Weaknesses to gain Opportunities, but they are just minors (36% only), and we will still work on them. We shall not leave them untreated there.

Ancient wisdom said that if you could not win over the Threats, you better avoid them. A more modern thoughts said that even if you could win over them, you better calculate your cost vs benefit, twice before do that.[37]

Productivity (especially for the CEO) is the benefit over resources cost ratio. So then winning the Threats on your Weaknesses (even if you are extremely lucky to achieve that), is definitely not a wise decision for CEO.

---

[36] *SWOT* analysis is a strategic planning method used to evaluate the Strengths, Weaknesses, Opportunities, and Threats involved in a project or in a business. http://www.en.wikipedia.org/wiki/**SWOT**_analysis

[37] To *Sun Tzu*, this meant to bring *victory* in the quickest, least bloody, least expensive to planning for *victory* in the most effective and *efficient* manners possible. http://www.**suntzu**blog.wordpress.com

0040. The Additional Second Life on the Remaining Age

Since you already get 267% capacity, it is 100% your first life, 100% your second life and 67% of your third life. Now you are an extremely very lucky person. While other pressed hard in rush time, you have the luxury to think about much more important future matters. You lead the time!

Most of the people in this world do not have ample time for work, neither for family and nor for personal life. A Gazelle must run every day to overrun the fastest Lion. A Lion must also running to outrun the slowest Gazelle. Whether they are Lion or Gazelle, they must run to live.[38]

What can the wealthy group of Lion solve this? They make a team work, led by the CEO. Their hunting plan explained, known by all members and every member is fully responsible for their specific function, to guard the strategic position. Some do frightening Gazelles and some others kill a Gazelle that enter the territory. They choose only one easiest when there are some Gazelle run to them. They only aiming other Gazelle, after left dead Gazelles a while safely. They must also do a very quick group lunch, since the larger group of Hyena (dogs) will always come to attack the Lion's (cats) hunting team, if the Lions take too much time for eating!

---

[38] "Every morning in Africa, a Gazelle wakes up. It knows it must run faster than the fastest lion or it will be killed. Every morning a Lion wakes up. It knows it must outrun the slowest Gazelle or it will starve to death. It doesn't matter whether you are a Lion or a Gazelle... when the sun comes up, you'd better be running."
http://www.thinkexist.com/quotation/every_morning_in.../298139.html

0041. 1st Benefit: More Time for Additional Pleasures

Becoming a CEO could be well paid, but also stress-full on the heavy responsibility. Is the CEO life being the only option you have? Don't you need other activities? Most of the people have personal life, aside from their CEO role. They live in family, social group and clubs, etc. Those are the common games people play[39]

In short, (1)Life is a place of Worship, (2)Life is a Place of Wealth and (3)Life is a place of Warfare. One can be a CEO for Wealth, but could also utilize it for Worship. Warfare could be done if some others threat the Wealth and /or Worship. Some people can live with just one or two of them, but most of the people did all of those three.[40]

So then the CEO Time Matrix, still also be useful for some haters of corporate animals and organization person's CEO types. Extinguishing (X-cross) the Unimportant and Irrelevant time wasters are always good for your life.

You better use (at least some of) the additional time gained for personal and amusement purposes. It's your life!

---

[39] *Erich Fromm*; Man's main task in life is to give birth to himself, to become what he potentially.
http://www.quotationspage.com/quotes/Erich_Fromm/

[40] The great eternal mystery human live is the sacred purpose as our mission in this life as the place for both: (1)Worship, (2)Wealth and (3)Warfare. In doing the Worship, we must do the ZIKR= Zerobase, Iman (Faith), Konsisten (Consistency) and R= Result Oriented.
http://www.amazon.com/Celestial-Management-Islamic-Wisdom-Beings/dp/1456450700;

0042. 2nd Benefit: Less Worrying Tight Scary Schedules

What? Scary tight schedules? That is common for any CEO's life. The reason is just one for them all. It is inability to decide things that are not Important for the organization and not Relevant to the CEO's role!

Most of the cases occur because inability to screen the activities of the CEO staffs, but in some significant cases those come from the inconsistency of CEO decisions. Saving 64% time by sacrificing 4% result now could make the CEO schedule be more pleasant, flexible and also productive. Now the CEO shall have more time to think and make better decisions than before.

How about many software's, palm-top, computers and small ICT (information and communication technology) helping tools? They are good only if you could Extinguish (X-cross) the unnecessary activities from the schedule.[41]

Best yet if you could Extinguish (X-cross) the unnecessary activities so you are free to concentrate on the business of your core CEO business, deadlines and special requests. Please be more flexible but effective at work.[42]

---

[41] Everyone wants to know their business is appreciated. Whether it is for your employees, sales team, partners, investors supplies or customers. http://www.lisasgiftwrappers.com/corporate_programs_lgw.php;

[42] The *CEO* may have bought in, but there has been plenty of opposition inside the *Flexible* work *schedules*, they say, heap needless bureaucracy on managers.
http://www.businessweek.com/magazine/content/06_50/b4013001.htm

0043. 3nd Benefit: Significant Productivity Improvement

By gaining 64% time less and just 4% performance less, then the remaining is 96% result for only 36% works. It could be 96% / 36% = 267% productivity or 267% - 100% = 167% additional capacity. If all of them also be reinvested on doing more for the organization.

This is a smarter way and a new approach on the common working activities. Work harder in the old style is impossible since the CEO had invested 100% of the time. We must do elimination to rebound in saturated "law of diminishing return's stage": Extinguish (X-cross) the 64%.[43]

Yes, in contrast to the common decreasing ratio of benefit over the cost, we better do the contrary (the other way around). Decreasing time resources by 64% will eliminate the total output by 4%, but the marginal output input ratio raised from 100% to 267%. It is a nice and winning game so far.

This is better because comes closer to the optimum productivity possible Mc = Mr (marginal cost = marginal revenue, intersection). It is not the maximum revenue, neither the maximum marginal cost, but the maximum productivity. In other words maximum output over input possible.[44]

---

[43] *law of diminishing returns* n. The tendency for a continuing application of effort or skill toward a particular project or goal to decline in.
http://www.answers.com › Library › Business & Finance

[44] The concept is important in microeconomics because a firm's optimal output (most profitable) is where its *marginal revenue* equals its *marginal cost*: http://www.moneyterms.co.uk/marginal-revenue/

0044. 4th Benefit: Better Priority Set for Future Cases

If you hold the present in your hand, by mastering yourself as CEO over the time (*chronos*), then it is most probably that you could even be better in the future.

Time to plan the future is essential. Carpenters better measure the log twice or trice, before cut it to lumber. Those are not vain. Supposing the log had been cut and it is still too long, then other cutting activities must be conducted. If the log had been cut and it is too short, all of the log will be less useful. Plan and measure them first, before make actions.[45]

The future is a mystery; we are obliged to use current information to predict the coming state that will not come about unless the predictions are correct.

We are now use the scientific 'Futurolog', and ancient people use 'Fortune Teller' to give informations for helping them preparing for the future. As the CEO, you are one of the most credible people that could work for the better future of the organization. So, please use this additional time as a pleasant weather for preparing the future.[46]

---

[45] What is the *purpose* and definition of a business *plan*? It defines where you want your business to be and how you want it to get there. http://www.business-**plan**-success.com/articles/business-**plan**-definition.php

[46] Dr. Pearson's profession isn't *fortune-telling* or clairvoyance; he is a prominent figure in the growing field of *futurology*. What is foresight/*futurology*? *Fortune Telling* or Intelligent Fortunes? http://www.vaultcareers.wordpress.com/tag/**futurology**

0045. 5th Benefit: Bringing More Confidence of Ability

Every person had the pride that must first set by self and then adjusted and affirmed by others (in the specific society). It could be over-estimated or under-estimated, but in general, other just makes minor adjustment on personal confidence initiated by the valuated person.[47]

Observations of empirical evidences show that more freedom brings better confidence to the person. A person with ample freedom could act independently and less limited by others. Those bring more confidence to the person. On the contrary determined and heavily told person had less of it.

What we have gain is 96% / 36% = 267% confidence of 267% - 100% = 167% additional self confidence. If the same principles also adopted by the lower person than CEO, the squad below and whole organization be confidence.

You could change the world if change yourself, organization, nation and region first (bottom-up). You will never could do it from top-down approach.

So, why are you still waiting? Let us start it now! A voyage of thousand miles, start with just a simple one step![48]

---

[47] *Confidence* is generally described as a state of being certain either that a hypothesis or prediction is correct or that a chosen course of action is the best or most. http://www.en.wikipedia.org/wiki/**Confidence**

[48] "A journey of *thousand mile* begins with a single *step*". (Un *voyage* de mille lieues commence toujours par un premier pas); Lao Tzu. http://www.forum.wordreference.com/showthread.php?t=1063547

0046. 6th Benefit: Better Resources from Giant Within

Sacrificing 4% is trivial, it just decreasing your performance to 96%. On the other hand, gaining 64% extra time is significant. More than that, you do not just get more timing, but also more research based philosophy.[49]

The benevolence wisdom gains from it are as follow:
1) You are the master of time, so take the control
2) You are really getting more time, since now on.
3) You are more independent from false myths!
4) Your decision quality is significantly improved
5) You had been more confident in decisiveness
6) You feel that decreasing 4% performance is OK
7) Your strategic and long range performance be better
8) Your subordinates see the changes and start follow
9) Your organization be more rational & productive

The proof of the pudding is in the eating. So, please go back to your CEO works and actually Extinguish (X-cross) 64% of the Unimportant and Irrelevant cases. See the difference. Please take a time to actually implement it in your real life before continue to the next chapter. Enjoy it![50]

---

[49] Before the modern idea of research emerged, we had a term for what philosophers used to call research as logical reasoning. So, it should come as no surprise that some of the basic distinctions in logic have carried over into contemporary research.
http://www.socialresearchmethods.net/kb/philosophy.php

[50] The key is to find the right *exercise* for you. If it is fun, you are more likely to stay motivated.
http://www.nlm.nih.gov/medlineplus/exerciseandphysicalfitness.html

CEO Time-Matrix

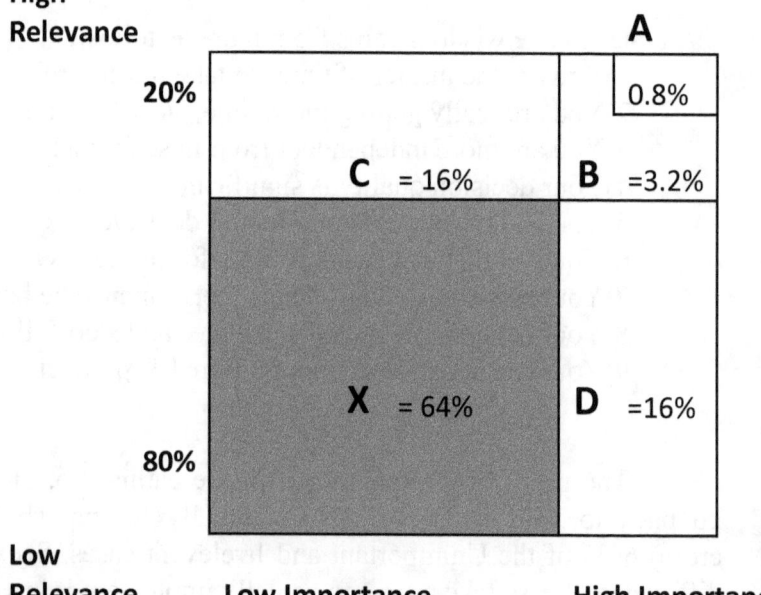

X (extinguished) quadrant= 80% x 80% = 64% works
The remaining time = 100% - 64% = 36%

X (extinguished) quadrant= 20% x 20% = 4% result
The remaining result = 100% - 4% = 96%

0048. **CHAPTER-III:**
   The D (Delegate), Quadrant (16% Less)

   After you had mastering the X (cross) or Extinguish quadrant, then you could work at 100% - (20% x 20%) = 96% excellence by using only 100% - (80% x 80%) = 36% resources. Your productivity becomes 95% / 36% =267%.

   Now it is the time to work on another Irrelevant works but this one is Important. Sound strange? Yes they are important but better done by other lower person than CEO. It means that you must assign subordinate to do it. IT saves 80% x 20% =16% for CEO time budget.

   Common problems might occur, because readiness of your subordinates might vary and needs different strokes:

(1)Some are ABLE and WILLING to do that, and then you could do DELEGATING for them to complete the task.

(2)Some are still UNABLE but WILLING to do that, so you must do SELLING to motivate them complete the task.

(3)Some are ABLE but UNWILLING to do that, so you must do PARTICIPATING to ensure them complete the task.

(4)The rest are UNABLE and UNWILLING to do that, so you must do TELLING to lead them complete the task.[51]

---

[51] The *Situational Leadership* Model was created by Ken Blanchard and Paul Hersey, and is probably the most used formal model of leadership today, http://www.leadertoday.org/faq/situational.htm

0049. Deleting All High Importance, but Low Relevance

Now the D (delegate) quadrant might save 80% x 20%= 16% more time, after the first 80% x 80% = 64% of X (cross) extinguish quadrant that we have discussed before in Chapter-II. So the total time saved had been 16% + 64% = 80%. Then the CEO could be focused only on Relevant matters with 100% - 16% - 64% = 20% working time. How about the result? Yes, following the standard Pareto's 80/20 statistics, the CEO could still enjoy 80% result from the 20% working time, after gaining extra 80% time!

The action in D (delegate) quadrant could give extra 16% time, but also sacrificing 16% results. Now the results had dropped from 96% to just 80%. Why do we still doing that when the quality Algebra still be square or even?

Because they gained 16% is for the CEO's time, which could be beneficial for the future of the organization. If done properly, D (delegating) action could empower subordinates and makes CEO get more freedom for improving results.

Key Success factor (KSF) here is that D (delegating) action, only could be assigned to the ABLE and WILLING subordinates, which normally are rare to find.[52] Never do D (delegating) action to UNABLE or UNWILLING subordinates, to avoid disaster of bad results.

---

[52] Principle in *Situational Leadership* is that leaders should adjust leadership styles to the followers' *readiness level* (ability & willingness); http://www.aboutiwp.com/Leadership%20and%20Coaching.pdf

0050. Save 80% x 20% = 16% of Potential Time Waster

One thing must be remember that on D (delegation) scheme; only the authority is given to the subordinate. The responsibility will still at the CEO as source of its power.[53] Intensive D (delegation) must be backed up by strong _control_[54] and _audits_[55] to make sure that the transfer of power were properly used by the representative. Absence of this important control will significantly downgrade the D (delegation) to just a dumping _laissez faire_ practices.[56]

The organization will be powerful if implementing D (delegation), control and audit properly on the _chained line of command_. It makes all members of the organization works together like an _organism_. In this sense, the (1) _unity of command_ and (2) _segregation of duties_, works. It also does regular check and rechecks to make sure that everything works well and corrective actions can be done quickly as needed.

---

[53] However the person who _delegated_ the work remains accountable for the outcome of the _delegated_ work.
http://www.en.wikipedia.org/wiki/Delegation

[54] _Control_ is the ability to purposefully direct, or suppress, change.
http://www.en.wikipedia.org/wiki/**Control**

[55] The general definition of an _audit_ is an evaluation of a person, organization, system, process, enterprise, project or product. The term most commonly refers to the financial aspects.
http://www.en.wikipedia.org/wiki/**Audit**

[56] _Laissez-Faire_, a French term that translates as "let things alone," originated in the eighteenth century with a school of French economists, known; http://_www.answers.com_ › _Library_ ›_Business & Finance_

0051. Only 20% Remaining, be 400% Bigger in Capacity

Now please count that the CEO had achieving 80% of the organizational targets, by just spending 20% of the time budget. If spending all the 100%, the result will be 80% x 100% /20% = 400% of the standard target.

So then the CEO could choose in between of 80% to 400% result for a number between 20% to 100% CEO time. Since every organization and every CEO are unique, then you could choose any appropriate portion on your favor.

Please learn the Pareto lesson from the simultan chess played by a famous Iranian Grand Master, against 604 tough players (some are junior and some others are more senior rated players). After 25 hours, the Grand Master wins over them by 590-6-8 (595 victory points) or the net of 582 chess points (>98.17%). It is a new and very efficient world record for 25 hours both in (1)Absolute victory points and (2)Relative percentage of the chess victory! Good job!

(1)How many chess victory points could any other better chess Grand Master make in 25 hours? Sure, less than 595. (2)How many % chess victory points could any other better chess Grand Master make in 25 hours? Sure, less than 98.17%. Yes, it is hard to get that from just 5 to 10 games![57]

---

[57] After 25 hours, the final results were 580 wins, 16 draws and 8 losses for a total score of 588 out of 604 or 97.35 percent. Ten more boards were added which he won but which were not counted for the record. http://www.fide.com/.../5055-world-record-604-board-**simultaneous-chess**

0052. Enjoy 300% Extra Time for More Opportunities

Please still be free to utilize the 0% up to 300% extra capacity gained for the best of your purposive CEO activities. It is not a mandatory to use all the 100% saved time.

Freedom itself is nice, but should be planned as proper. Less planning will make freedom be a peril more than grace. Please use it wisely to optimize your performances.[58] Even though people feels trapped in the busy schedules, its contrast of no schedule is also torturing. What people really need is just freedom to choose among options.

Further decision making studies also said that sudden freedom brings too much alternatives that could even makes the decision worse. Just two or three options are better.[59]

Sports, leisure and mental spiritual or even martial arts will also bring better wealth, health and breath. They also need to be composed as proper, since too much or less than needed will not be good for your life as a total.[60]

---

[58] The *escape from freedom* also finds "the need to be related to the world outside oneself, the need to avoid aloneness." Religious extremes. http://www.alternativeinsight.com/**Escape_from_freedom**.html

[59] *Decision* making is the study of identifying and choosing *alternatives* based on the values. *Too much* information can actually reduce the quality of a *decision*. http://www.virtualsalt.com/crebook5.htm

[60] Ballet dancers have it. So do serious practitioners of pilates, tai chi, and yoga. Those who sit parked in front of computer screens all day? Not so well. http://www.articles.boston.com/.../29574829_1_tai-chi-posture-notebook-comp

0053. The Third to Fifth Life on the Remaining Age

How about a deep lake skill? Is that possible? Normal person are commonly a '_deep well_' specialist. They know one special thing in depth and get well paid because of it.[61]

When time changed, specialized skills become obsolete and replaced by new technologies. The specialist persons then get fired and could not survive like powerful dinosaur after the ice ages. They become extinct![62]

Then come the group of '_shallow lake_' generalist,[63] who could flexibly survive in any field. They know almost every subject, but not so deep because of their learning time limit. Now, they also had a sunset because of the 'Google' and other Information and Communication Technologies (ICT). Now Bangalore the Indian Silicon Valley takes a lead.

How could you be the '_deep lake_' to survive this more global world? Yes, by using Pareto's 80/20 statistics. Learn as many 80% Excellencies as possible by the 20% resources!

---

[61] One who is devoted to a particular occupation or branch of study or research: "_Specialists_ tend to think in grooves" (Elaine Morgan). http://www.thefreedictionary.com/**specialis**

[62] A _change_ in temperature sparks a mass _dinosaur_ migration, but causes problems for smaller breeds. http://www.youtube.com/watch?v=MtWOBYf19gg

[63] _Generalist_ may refer to: a person with a wide array of knowledge, the opposite of which is a specialist. http://www.en.wikipedia.org/wiki/**Generalist**

0054. 1st Benefit: More Time for Additional Pleasures

Having pleasures itself is a pleasure. Also having options to choose is another pleasure. Owning ample free time can always be pleasant. Knowing many efficient options could add them all. Oh, what a wonderful world![64]

Everyday is a beautiful day. Have you ever telling yourself about how nice is a blue sky? How fantastic are the green trees for the climate and your eyes. What a beautiful panoramic view of the seas and mountains. There are the, always be there, but you did not always have time to appreciate them all. Not it is the time, enjoy it now![65]

D (delegating) actions might improve your chances to see this world in a very different way. Does it exciting?

The 300% capacity gain will more beneficial at CEO level. The higher a person and the more strategic and greater impact is the position, the greater advantage they get from this 300% additional capacity or a total of 400% possibility.

Since lower position deals with more technical and mechanical matters, they enjoy this idea less than the top guy.

---

[64] "What a *Wonderful World*" is a song written by Bob Thiele (as George Douglas) and George David Weiss. It was first recorded by Louis Armstrong and released.
http://www.en.wikipedia.org/wiki/What_a_Wonderful_World

[65] *Thanksgiving* Day is a holiday celebrated primarily in the United States and Canada. Traditionally, it has been a time to give thanks to God, friends, and family. http://www.en.wikipedia.org/wiki/Thanksgiving

0055. 2nd Benefit: Less Worrying Tight Scary Schedules

If you do practicing D (delegation) from time to time, then you could identify which subordinates that could be assigned for more duties successfully. Even same subordinate will also growing on their learning curves to make the CEO and organizational live better and easier as well.

Supposing that the CEO already have more capable candidates to be D (delegated), and then lot options could be done. It even could do simultaneous presences at same time (that a single CEO is impossible to perform). It grows better.

Things that are also important here are turnover and dependencies. If only the CEO can do it, then the CEO will be very tired and the organization could not grow well. If some others can do that, the whole organization is safer.

Lots of personal reason makes people comes in and out the organization (turnover). If the members are unrotatable and irreplaceable then the organization could not grow well. Like in the US Marine, members could die, move out or replaced by others, but organization must go onward. Duty, discipline, hierarchy and organizational honor![66]

---

[66] For U.S. Marines of any faith who may desire guidance when contacting their Maker, the Marine Corps has a ready aid, The *Marine's Prayer*: Grant me the courage to be proficient in my daily performance. Keep me loyal and faithful to my superiors and to the duties my country and the Corps have entrusted to me. Make me considerate of those committed to my leadership. Help me to wear my uniform with dignity, and let it remind me daily of the traditions which I must uphold. http://www.usmcpress.com/heritage/**marines_prayer**.htm

0056. 3rd Benefit: Significant Productivity Improvement

Long before Samuel F.B. Morse found the telegraph cable, many African tribes could send message quickly for thousands of miles by rhythm of drums sound code. Similar things used for the early telegraph. What lesson could we learn from both of the successful systems?[67]

Yes, the D (delegating) method, based on commonly understood shared values, from one trusted person to another. Since the CEO could not be presence at many places at the same time as limited by possibility and efficiency, then delegating Important job to many subordinates is essential.

The history has told us what happen before and after them and how could those make a difference for military and social purposes thereafter. Time saving and productivity!

World ancient history had proven that even a nomad small tribe could hold the world in their hands if using D (delegating) principles as proper. Mongolian postal[68] could quickly send from Turkey to Beijing or Ulan Bator. So they could consolidate their troops very quickly at their age and gaining almost impossible victories against richer kingdoms.

---

[67] *Samuel* Finley Breese *Morse*, inventor of several improvements to the telegraph, was born in Charlestown, Mass. on April 27, 1791.
http://www.web.mit.edu/invent/iow/**morse**.html

[68] The *Mongols* also used the *postal relay* stations to host visiting envoys, to provide them with escorts, food, and shelter, and, most important, to guarantee their speed. http://www.silk-road.com/artl/pax**mongo**lica.shtml

0057. 4th Benefit: Better Priority Set for Future Cases

The eye of CEO as the C-in-C (*commander in chief*) has a longer range of vision than the rest of the organization. He got the current information better, so then CEO must concentrate to solve the future's potential problems.[69]

Problem identification and preventive solutions need more energy, so then the CEO must be freed from daily routine activities, in order to get better future preparation.[70]

The D (delegating) activities are mostly repeated again and again and suppose to be done by many peoples. So then the comprehensive SOP[71] (*standard operating procedures*), those are definitely needed for some most frequent regular activities possible. It uses Pareto's statistics.

Last but not least: D (delegations) needs bold and consistent *reward and punishment* system, like the widely known *stick and carrot* method to give *incentives* to desired behavior and *disincentives* to the unfavorable behaviors.

---

[69] Leaders have vision. They share a dream and direction that other people want to share and follow. The *leadership vision* goes beyond your written. http://www.humanresources.about.com/od/**leadership**/a/**leader_vision**.htm

[70] This article presents seven powerful tools and techniques you can use to prevent problems throughout your organization. The primary key to *problem prevention;* http://www.positive-way.com/business/**problem**.htm

[71] The terms *standard operating procedure* or *SOP*, is used in a variety of different contexts, such as healthcare, education, industry or the military. http://www.en.wikipedia.org/wiki/**Standard_operating_procedure**

0058. 5th Benefit: Bringing More Confidence of Ability

Ability is the potential power, only employed when needed. Power itself also is a work potential. Then in short: ability is the working capacity of person and organization. On CEO cases, it involves more organizational potential than at the lower level. It is assumed the CEO knows the organizational resources and capabilities (might be in business and /or military) better than others.

It is expected that the confidence of the CEO should be based more on SWOT (*strengths, weaknesses, opportunities* and *threats*), rather than on the situational personal emotions. Total consciousness is definitely needed for quality decisions. How about its result?

Decision result could be correct of imperfect. Nobody knows it in the beginning. Empirical research said that rational and prepared decision is much better than just *gut-feelings*. Timely decision is better than anachronism (false timing) one.

Experience of the CEO is superior for solving repeated problems, but analytical ability is much more useful to handle totally new and strange situations.

Using STAR model (*situation, target, actions* and *recommendation*), results better for the bottom-up suggestion. Those comes from trusted delegated subordinated to be finally decided by the CEO, that could reject them but could not be the regular initiator of the large organizational routine (daily) decisions, that just need to be reviewed regularly.

0059. 6th Benefit: Better Resources from Giant Within

There is a hero, deep inside yourself. If you have ample time to know yourself better, this giant will feed you positive ideas, then you becomes bigger and bigger from day to day.[72] On the contrary, if you feed the giant with negative ideas, then you becomes smaller and smaller from day to day.

The organization will face a serious problem if the CEO did not growing. This example will easily be copied by the crowd and the organization also become weaker. Life is not fair, because *bad ideas done and copied much faster* compared to the good one (especially if exaggerated).[73]

Most of the people that are believing God almighty agreed that you must work hard to achieve the best of your destiny which is programmed in IF THEN format. So the decision is yours and depends on your D (delegating) quality.

On the contrary, for those who do not believe in God; They must work on their own destiny since they are not sure whether God is existing. So, whoever you are (whether you are a God believer or Atheist), you must and better work on your destiny, based on your *circle of influence* and *circle of concern.* Two circles that shape your rationality and idealism.

---

[72] Awaken the *Giant Within* : How to Take Immediate Control of Your Mental, Emotional, Physical and Financial Destiny! by *Anthony Robbins* Paperback; http://www.amazon.com/Awaken-**Giant-Within-**Immediate.../0671791540

[73] A *positive mental attitude* creates a mindset of abundance, enthusiasm, and solutions. Instead of thinking about what can't be done. http://www.en.wikipedia.org/wiki/**Positive_mental_attitude**

CEO Time-Matrix

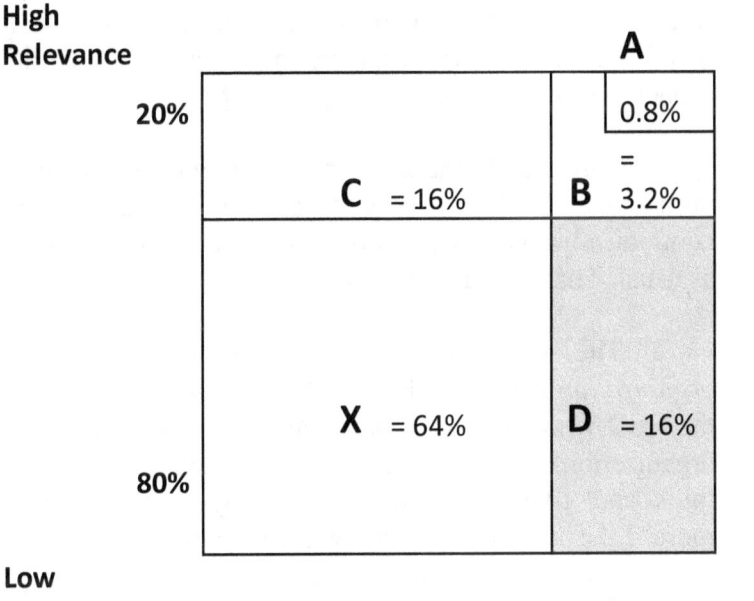

D (delegated) quadrant= 80% x 20% = 16% works
The remaining time = 100% - 64% - 16% = 20%

D (delegated) quadrant= 20% x 80% = 16% result
The remaining result = 100% - 4% - 16% = 80%

~ 60 ~

0061.　**CHAPTER-IV:**
C (Contingency), or Filing Quadrant (16% Less)

Please count your blessing (count them one-by-one) so far. You already get 80% extra time (X-cross and D-delegating) and just sacrifice 20% result less. Then it is 80% result from just 20% time or resources used. In other words it is 80%/20% = 400% capacity now, or 300% additional capacity or time gains.

Surprisingly there are so many CEOs in this world fell proud that 'they' had worked very hard. That is already a common mistake: CEO works hard and organization works as usual. That is totally wrong![74]

The main function of CEO is to '*make the organization works*", achieving better than targeted! It is not the CEO who must work hard, but every other person in the organization! The role of the CEO is to lead; means analyze, think and give clear direction for organization to achieve more! Like a conductor leading music in the orchestra.[75]

Let us go to the next step: C (contingency) quadrant!

---

[74] Finally, the award for hardest-working CEO, or the designation as the guy most in need of a vacation, goes to Lockheed Martin's (LMT) Robert Stevens. Last year, Stevens received about $35,000 in "other compensation" to pay for vacation time that he didn't take.
http://www.usatoday.com/money/.../2008-04-09-ceo-perks-pay_N.htm

[75] Typically, the **CEO** has responsibilities as a communicator, decision maker, leader, and manager. The communicator **role** can involve the press and the rest of society.
http://www.en.wikipedia.org/wiki/Chief_executive_officer

0062.   Deleting All High Relevance, but Low Importance

Having proper legal evidence and ample documentary support is Relevant to the role of CEO, but to work on it is not Important! What CEO must preset and consistently follow is make a strong filing system an alphabetic basis.[76]
No CEO ever expecting that any authority will ask for that file. The wish that it shall never been called or asked ever. But no CEO is willing to take risk that they could have absence of that document when needed most by the authority.

So it is C (contingent) quadrant, not Important but very much relevant to the CEO role. Off course the CEO do not have to file those by themselves, but must keep the strong file securely, easy to Retrieve. All the Records must have the Right place and filed in a systematic way. (3R must done).

Utilizing alphabetic system will be better if the filing will be kept for longer than one month time. The date and other numbers will be forgotten faster than relevant file name. That is the reason why the military, intelligence and sciences used encyclopedia and dictionary to retrieve long data or information stored. They are not Important but Relevant! So the CEO must have secured quickly Retrievable C (contingent) strong Relevant file, close to them.[77]

---

[76] **Alphabetic Filing** alphabetic systems group documents together by letters of the name from A - Z. These systems can be used for any volume of records. http://www.deskdemon.com/pages/uk/information/skills/mfile

[77] Paper Tiger **Document** Management and **Filing System** Software has helped us out a lot at work. This simple indexing system for the hanging files in our filing. http:// www.thepapertiger.com/

0063. Save 80% x 20% = 16% of Potential Time Waster

Contingent (C) plan and its preventive preparation is very Relevant to the CEO role. It is just a filing system, so set a best useful one and follow it consistently. No additional works needed there. We could review and reclassify them later if we have ample 'non-busy' time to do it in the future.

How much time could you save by 'no work' and rely it to the filing system? It is 20% x 80% = 16% additional time saving after 64% of X (extinguish) and 16% of D (delegate) quadrant. So then they are a total of 64% + 16% + 16% = 96% time savings. Only 4 % time that CEO really must work by themselves.

This will make CEO life much easier! Performance might also be 80% x 20% = 16% less or totally decreased by 4% + 16% + 16% = 36% or remains 100% - 36% = 64%, but that come from just 4% of CEO efforts! It is productive at 64% / 4% = 16 times or 1600%!

Let us take the accounting C (contingent) liabilities like bank guarantee as the example. It is yet not a bank debt to any other parties, but the bank must keep it in the strong C (contingent) file. It could become a direct bank liability, if and only if, the guaranteed customer fails to perform the agreed performance standard as required.[78]

---

[78] **Contingent liabilities** are possible future liabilities that will only become certain on the occurrence of some future event. A **contingent liability** is less certain.
http://www.moneyterms.co.uk/**contingent_liabilities**/

0064. Only 4% Remaining, be 1600% Bigger in Capacity

Let go back to its Algebra for a while, so the CEO just work by 4% effort, but resulting 64% proceeds. The efficiency is 64% / 4% = 16 times compared to the common 100% /100% while most of CEOs ratio is smaller than 100%. The 16 times is 1600% and there is 1600% -100%= 1500% additional capacity gains from deleting X, D and C quadrants.

In other words; if CEO could achieve 64% result by only 4% efforts, it is just need to do 4% x 100% / 64% = 6.25% efforts to get the 100% performance back. The remaining CEO time is 100% - 6.25% = 93.75%. If it is reinvested in the business = 93.75% / 6.25% = 15 times or 1500% extra times for doing works and gaining more results.

Like we have discussed before in X-cross (extinguish) and D (delegating) quadrant, you do not have to reinvest the total of your 1500% resources gained. Just give it in between 0% to 1500% as proper according to your comfort level. At least, now you have more and better options for it.

What is Relevant to CEO role (although not Important to be worked) here is that "never left the C (contingencies)". If you seriously work on it you will miss the important task. That is common because people prefer to do nice jobs than doing the unpleasant but important jobs.[79]

---

[79] This is not to say that you won't be back: doing a **good job** on the first project. Though some consultants (**like** me) **prefer** a solitary work-at-home existance. Ongoing business is much more **important than** maximizing every billable hour. http://www.unixwiz.net/techtips/be-consultant.html

0065. Enjoy 1500% Extra Time for More Opportunities

The extra 1500% time resources mean that you already have 16 times CEO capacity than before. You could use the time for additional productivity, leisure or increasing your capability for preparing the future duties.[80]

Quality control in this CEO time management is a continuous improvement activity. Everything could still be improved. Even the most excellent and efficient one could still becomes better and better. The race for quality is the road that never ends. Sky is the limit.[81]

Please be ready for new opportunities that you had never imagined before. Now you are almost a totally new person that could do strange things you never done. There is nothing to lose, because you already achieving more than 100%, before you try to do new things. So then it is a journey, and knowledge building experiences to make a good use of the new capacity found.[82]

---

[80] **Leadership** can be viewed as being defined by the job: (a)Executive – Coordinating group activities and overseeing the setting of policies, (b) Planner – Deciding how the group will achieve its goals, (c) Policy maker – Establishing policies and goals. http://www.*changingminds.org* › *Disciplines › Leadership › Leadership actions*

[81] **Quality** - The **race** for **quality** has no finish line so technically it's more like a death march. http://www.luceperformancegroup.com/Funny-Motivational

[82] A successful executive and family man takes up jogging for a hobby. Soon his desire to excel as a long distance runner interferes with his career and marriage. http://www.imdb.com/title/tt0145459/

0066. The Additional Sixth to Fifteenth of CEO Life

Traditional person have their own spiritual relaxation. While the western had a "*born again*"[83] phenomena, the eastern world had "*reincarnation*"[84] dreams and the Middle East had the "*tafakur*"[85] for establishing new spiritual life.

These chances are extremely luxury, not so many people in this world could enjoy them. They miss to communicate to the most important person in earth; they themselves. That is silly, since additional time is the charity from the very deep of you yourself. Please never be too cruel for the best of yours.[86]

The journey within yourself and to know the very deep of you yourself is also Relevant, Important and Interesting. Please do not miss this rare opportunity.

---

[83] In Christianity, **born again** refers to a "spiritual rebirth" (regeneration) of the human soul or spirit, contrasted with the physical birth everyone experiences.
http://www.en.wikipedia.org/wiki/**Born_again**_(Christianity)

[84] **Reincarnation**: Believing in second chances - One in ten Americans remembers living a past life; What evidence is there.
http://www.cbsnews.com/stories/2011/05/15/sunday/main20063019.shtml

[85] **Tafakur**, or reflective thought; an endeavor that is required of every believer, secrets behind secrets of the Naqshbandi sufi way Shaykh Nazim Haqqani deputy Shaykh Hisham Kabbani Islamic order.
http://www.nurmuhammad.com/.../naqshbandimeditationillustration.htm

[86] I found the **greatest love** of all. Inside of me. The **greatest love** of all. Is easy to achieve. Learning to love **yourself**. It is the **greatest love** of all.
http://www.azlyrics.com/lyrics/whitneyhouston/**greatestlove**ofall.html

0067. 1st Benefit: More Time for Additional Pleasures

What is the pleasure? It is the personal experience in thing that you like and even still enjoy for the longer period than the tenure of its actual stimulus. They are very nice.[87]

Those bring happiness, if the performance is better than expected. Please be extremely careful with this. Very high expectation could make good things less than expected and makes people unhappy. In order to be always happy, a person must optimize performances but keep the expectations low or at least on the common realistic level.

The role is (H= P-E), happiness is the performances less by the expectations. When the value is positive, people will feel happy but if the value is negative they will feel sad. In percentage is (H%= P/E -100%) for the relative ratios.[88]

Most of the advices said that you could have a big dream and then it will come true. If you have no dream, your dream will not come true. Wrong! It just a myth. It is better for you to have a big performance at whatever dream level you might have. The better performance is worth better and the smaller or more realistic your preset dream, will make your sadness less lethal. Then you shall get better safety.

---

[87] **Pleasure** describes the broad class of mental states that humans and other animals experience as positive, enjoyable, or worth seeking. It includes more specific feelings.
http://www.en.wikipedia.org/wiki/**Pleasure**

[88] Amazon.com: **Arigato**, Obrigado... (Thanks): Portuguese-Japan 1550-1647 Historic Novel (9781453786369): Steve **Asikin**: Books.
http://*www.amazon.com* › *Books* › *Literature & Fiction*

0068. 2nd Benefit: Less Worrying Tight Scary Schedules

Please evaluate your target and achievement schedule again, especially after you eliminate X-cross (extinguish), D (delegating) and C (contingent) quadrants of the total 64% + 16% +16% = 96% Pareto's statistical savings of CEO time.

Tight scary schedule will not be good for your life. You most try to get-out from the common human trap; desire and suffering. Human destiny is to feel sad and suffering.[89]

It does not matter to have nothing. That is common in every body's life. Problem comes if you want something, but you still have nothing! It is desires that create suffering, neither the bad conditions nor condition of have nothing itself.[90]

It is very common that our mental creates meaning from every sadness and happiness we have. Most of people experiencing sadness more frequent than happiness in life. It is not because of frequencies of bad things occurring, but mostly because of their wrong unrealistic expectation about life.[91]

---

[89] We normally view happiness and **sadness** to be opposites on a single continuum, but I propose that it is time to change. http://www.the-mouse-trap.com/.../happiness-opposed-to-despairennui-**sadness**

[90] By watching people **Buddha** found out that the **causes** of **suffering** are craving and desire, and ignorance. http://www.**buddha**net.net/e-learning/**buddhism**/bs-s04.htm

[91] Not that long ago, there were nights I went to sleep in strange places praying I wouldn't wake up. After another night of bad decisions.

0069. 3nd Benefit: Significant Productivity Improvement

People are normally concern about many things they could not actually control. You could see so many discussion in television and internet that people very much angry about things outside their controlling ability. It is useless but real. They waste their time and energies in vain.[92]

CEO productivity will increase if the organization concentrates on its *'Circle of Influence'* and not wasting much of their times at the interesting *"Circle of Concern"*. Productivity is measured by achievement we made that is useful in reality, and not as the intellectual gymnastic.[93]

We could not control the sudden impulses come to our brain. They are almost 50 thousands a day.[94] What we should really control is our *'response'* not just *'reaction"*. It is a very smart and conscious move, does analyzing first: choosing its best alternative before carefully responding.[95]

---

http://www.newsfeed.time.com/.../rangers-fan-tragedy-**more-sadness**-for-josh

[92] The Age **Concern discussion** boards provide a space to discuss anything from health to holidays and computers to care homes. http://www.ageuk.org.uk/chat

[93] The problems, challenges, and opportunities fall into two areas--**Circle** of **Concern** and **Circle** of **Influence**. Proactive people focus efforts on the influence. https://www.stephencovey.com/7habits/7habits-habit1.php

[94] Atrophy/death of neurons, 50000 **per day** (between ages 20 and 75). The total **information** processing activity of the **brain** is hard to estimate. http://www.vadim.oversigma.com/MAS862/Project.html

0070. 4th Benefit: Better Priority Setting of Future Cases

CEO must try to organize their mind first, before could implementing their personal ideas on organizational level. Neat and systematic mind does help in managing or commanding others for collective performances.[96] In order to lead the organization effectively, the CEO must be the person with string internal control. They could be independent or inter dependent, but not a dependent person that could be controlled by the external power.[97]

Better priority setting on future potential problems could be done by the CEO that had already freed from X-cross (extinguish), D (delegated) and C (contingent) quadrant of actions as they perform 64% resulted from 4% time used. CEO has so many staffs and subordinate to do routine and regular activities. CEO only needed in strategic, futuristic potential problem and irregular problem solving.

By guarding the organization from the future danger, the CEO could be more effective. In most cases *contingency* and *succession plan* makes organizational future be better.

---

[95] That's why it is so easy to go into a downward spiral without apparent hope of survival. We now also have to distinguish **response** from **reaction**. http://www.help-my-relationship.com.s31408.gridserver.com/

[96] **Harry Lorayne's** Secrets of Mind Power: How to **Organize** and Develop the Hidden Powers of Your Mind. http://www.amazon.com/s?...**organize**...n%3A283155%2Ck%3Aorganiz e%

[97] Balancing **External** and **Internal Control**. Behavior-based safety is founded on a principle that behavior is directed by preceding events. http://www.safetyperformance.com/.../Balancing**External**and**Internal**Co ntrol

0071. 5th Benefit: Bringing More Confidence of Ability

Capable CEOs will be more confidence than others, because they know ample skills and information,[98] Relevant to their roles and Important to their organization. Incapabilities will make them depends on other people and could not make the organization be performing.[99]

Personal intelligence shown by CEO will be the example that other subordinates copy and follow. First function of CEO is *establishing direction* or *path finding*. Then *role modeling* and *aligning* the rest of organization. The CEO must make sure that no one uses the resources for achieving thing which is not needed by the organization.[100]

CEO also must make the organization work smart at its '*core competence*' and use its resources efficiently. Modern world had plenty of allies and '*out-sourcing specialist*' that could perform hard jobs faster and cheaper.[101]

---

[98] "**Confidence** is the **ability** to feel beautiful without needing someone to tell you first, but smiling when someone does!" http://www.twitter.com/Golden_Barbie/status/15857900944

[99] Concentration - **ability** to maintain focus; **Confidence** - believe in one's abilities; Control - **ability** to maintain emotional control regardless of distraction. http://www.brianmac.co.uk/psych.htm

[100] If there's one thing start-up **CEOs** have to excel at it's managing the **alignment** of interests across a ton of different people. http://www.instigatorblog.com/startup-**ceos**-masters-of-**alignment**

[101] **core competency** of an organization should not be **outsourced**. Anything not a **core competency** is then con- sidered a viable **outsourced**. http://www.decisionsciences.org/decisionline/vol29/29_4/info_29_4.pdf

0072. 6th Benefit: Better Resources from Giant Within

There is a giant of very big potential inside of you. Even though it is till limited, it is far beyond the wildest dreaming that you ever imaging. To make it simpler and clearly understood, some writer said that it is almost unlimited.[102]

Anthony Robbins at page 59, notes 72 in this book said that this giant within you is now sleeping. You need to awaken it, by throwing X-cross (extinguish), D (delegating), and C (contingency) quadrants. Only after the CEO drops those three, the brighter future opportunity comes closer.

Now you had eliminate 64% + 16% +16% = 96% unnecessary time of yours. So then by doing just 100% - 64% -16% -16% = 4%, you still get 100% - 4% -16% - 64% result. Your CEO productivity has been increased to 64% / 4% = 1600% or multiplied by 16 times. You had won the 1600% - 100% = 1500% or 15 times your original capacity more!

Here you could and must congratulate yourself for that significantly great improvement, and then please be prepared for an even better or more drastic advancement for it. Now, please take your time, make a deep breath and prepare your mental ground for the next step. We will seriously sharpen your new 15 times capacity gain soon.

---

[102] SET YOUR GOALS HIGH...THEN EXCEED THEM! Millions of people throughout the world have improved their lives using **The Magic of Thinking Big**. Dr. David J. Schwartz. http://www.amazon.com/**Magic-Thinking-Big**-David.../dp/0671646788

CEO Time-Matrix

High
Relevance

A

20%   0.8%

C = 16%   B =3.2%

80%   X = 64%   D = 16%

Low
Relevance

Low Importance   High Importance
80%   20%

C (contingency) quadrant= 20% x 80% = 16% works
The remaining time = 100% - 64% - 16% -16% = 4%

C (contingency) quadrant= 80% x 20% = 16% result
The remaining result = 100% - 4% - 16% -16% = 64%

0074. **CHAPTER-V:**
B (Book-Later), Delayed Quadrant (3.2% Less)

We have left X-cross (extinguish), D (delegating) and C (contingency) quadrant so far those had reduced = 64% + 16% + 16% = 96% unnecessary CEO works. The remaining CEO time that will manage= 100% - 64% - 16% -16% = 4%. What is the Pareto 80/20 statistics here? Urgency forces![103]

Why do we still discussing the urgency here? Why don't we do it much earlier at X, D or C quadrants? Yes, after all at the individual level on top of the organizational pyramid, the CEO must still manage individual schedules.

It is interesting that most of the individual time could also be B (booked) to be done later. We just tickler system like we have discussed before on page 32-33 of this book, They consist of remaining agenda for 1)direct activities or also 2)schedule to review old tickler and make revision for later works of planning session.

How much time for this B (book later) activities? As Pareto's statistic proposed it s 80% x 20% x20% = 80% x 4% = 3.2%. Then the remaining activities that urgently must be done by the CEO themselves is 20% x 4% = 0.8% which could also be resulted from 4% - 3.2% = 0.8% of total time.

Now we could clearer see that B (book time later) is 80% of the real 4% CEO time or 3.2% from the total time.

---

[103] a)The quality or condition of being urgent; pressing importance: the **urgency** of the call for help; pleading with **urgency**. b)A pressing necessity. http://www.thefreedictionary.com/**urgency**

0075. High Importance, High Relevance Not Urgent

Please keep be consider that the activities in B (book time later) quadrant is Important, and Relevant to be the most of CEO effective time. It should be not urgent to make CEO performs better. Ample time is definitely needed and no rush is very much needed for CEO to make better decision.[104]

We do not mean that this B (book time later) quadrant should also be left like the other by thrown CEO activities in X-cross (extinguish), D (delegating), and C (contingency) quadrants. CEO definitely must do work in this 4% remaining quadrant, but 80% of them could be planned and no significant urgency might happen to a well prepared CEO.

Most of CEO real activity must on this B (book time later) quadrant, and only on 20% remaining CEO time or 0.8% of the total time given to be done by CEO in a hurry. The main job of CEO is Important and Relevant, but no urgent. CEO only do urgent work if nothing other possible.

CEO sits on top of the organizational pyramid and should focus only to strategic and long term organizational objectives. Only sudden and unexpected significant changes that could make CEO trapped in urgency. Most of the CEO job normally could be planned long before and the rest could be scheduled to B (book time later).

---

[104] I think the most important **CEO task** is defining the course that the business will set a broad direction, and also to take particular **decisions** along the way. http://www.woopidoo.com › *Business Quotes* › *Famous Managers*

0076. Save 80% x 4% = 3.2% of Potential Time Waster

If this B (book time later) quadrant done as proper (not thrown away), the CEO could work in a more effective way. It is good to have the diary, but the more important is how to write properly to make your diary work effectively.

Is there any different in writing on diary for CEO and common person? Yes, definitely. How? Common people noting at diary on the schedule of actual event (i.e. today) to record everything nicely and hopefully accurately.[105]

On the contrary CEO better noting actual inputs on one day before the next schedule due, to be reviewed there and preparing the actual event carefully. If the activity is for the next two months, it must be recorded today but on one day before next two months' page. Nothing could be missed!

Most of the people will forget things they write in their diary, so do us. Supposing we noting the activities on our diary based on the relevant due date, then the diary is not just blank when we open activities scheduled for tomorrow or next two days. The diary will lead us and guide us accurately.

It just needs to do small changes in our diary noting activities, but that give us big beneficial guidance to prepare and perform our future activities significantly better.

---

[105] The word "journal" may be sometimes used for "**diary**," but generally a **diary** has (or intends to have) daily entries, whereas journal-**writing** can be less frequent. http://www.en.wikipedia.org/wiki/Diary

0077.   Only 0.8% Rest, be 12500% Bigger Capacity

If this B (book time later) quadrant is consistently maintained and regularly reviewed. The CEO could achieve many things more than before. When CEO open the individual diary, activities planned for today, tomorrow and day after tomorrow are properly recorded in useful; and timely format.

In today's world, the electronic diary technology had been advanced at very useful format. Google Calendar, i-pad, organized communicator, black berry, palm-top, lap-top and note book computers are easy to find at reasonable prices.

Very confidential original legal documents could be sent thru personal assistant and adjutant. Less confidential could use professional courier and document delivery services. If it is not so formal but need to be quickly sent, then you could use email for private and fax for public.

Now, the email could also be read easily to communicator and black berry. SMS (short message services) could be used for quick confidential simple correspondence. Call only when it is urgent but do not need in depth reactions.

SMS is better than phone calls for complex discussion because do not need mutual coincidence of serious deep thoughts discussion. Sender and receiver could send message as quickly as possible at their comfort time. It does not need online real time connection of shallow inaccurate speeches.[106]

---

[106] **SMS Benefits** An SMS is personal Unlike an e-mail, an SMS is much more likely to be read by a person at any one time. http://www.visualgsm.com/wire_sms_topic02.htm

0078. Enjoy the 12400% Extra Time for Opportunities

If you could do this B (book time later) quadrant as proper, only 10% - 64% - 16% -16% -3.2%= 0.8% works done is urgency. You capability had grown to 100% / 0.8% = 12500% or 125 times, then you have 12400% extra time. It is yours, unless you abdicate them to someone else. Be careful!

Please try to answer this question: "What kind of phone that prisoners use to communicate between them?" What? Yes, you know that: "Cell-phone!?". You are correct!

Is that funny? Anything strange there? Yes. Your Cellular-phone is also a cell-phone! Although it is not means as Jail-phone like above, it makes you tied, trap and caught arrested almost in very similar meaning. It pushes you.

It makes you activities pushed until you have less or inadequate independent schedule for yourself. You always pick them up immediately when they ring. Sad fully some of them will ring endlessly 24 hours a day, 365 days a year!

Using SMS and Email will help you reduce its forces, but set a time, an hour a day to make all your calls is better. Never pick them up, unless the caller already be given your approval before or very shocking news sent by family.[107]

---

[107] The Do Not **Disturb** function stops any incoming **calls** from ringing on your **phone**. When activated, callers will be sent directly to your voice mail. http://www.ist.mit.edu/services/telephony/voip/userguide/dnd

0079. Twenty Fifth to A Hundred Twenty Fourth Life

Similar like the phone management, you only could be reached by people if and only if you had approved them before. Try to make a quick escaping clause, say polite excuse and immediately run away from unscheduled person.

You only communicate to people when you like it, and make yourself hard to be reached and quickly escaping when caught by coincidence. This is strange and funny but you will enjoy it well. I give you much more freedom that you had ever imagined as a normal person.

Please do not be a standing target. As CEO, always make yourself mobile, hard to be followed by CEO of other organization. Please position yourself as unique person.[108]

"Once upon a time a healthy CEO politely forced to have a conversation with unneeded person of same clan. It is impolite to refuse him but it is bad to make the CEO works for the village person's schedule. The CEO then decides to keep warm welcome but use stairway to climb to his office at the skyscraper. The unneeded person is following but could not climb more than six floors. So then CEO walks alone to the security door and the unneeded parson could not follow the nice CEO to come inside the screened secured office."

---

[108] I had a **salesman** approach me once as I was mowing the lawn. I told him I did not see. They are already being rude by injecting themselves into your life and **disturbing** your peace.
http://www.neoseeker.com/forums/879/t1625819-intentionally-disturbing/

0080. 1st Benefit: More Time for Additional Pleasures

As a CEO, you might have been hunted news makers and *paparazzi* that seriously disturbing your life. You better B (book time later) for press conference, with excellent price release printed and ample food. Most of them will go to the party tables with the printed matter and never come closer.[109]

So then they just approaching to make quick pictures and while you want to make bold statements that make your organization different than any others. Question and answer forum will be great if you are a quick thinker. It is colossal, monumental and they must wait for others before asking.

If there are already nothing to say, you better be nice and inviting them to take snacks and slipped-out quietly. Say apologies that you must go to another place that moment.

Press relation is one of the most Important CEO job, but CEO does not have to meet them all the time. It is because as the head of organization, CEO must also have a flexible time to perform the job creatively.

Use at least two postal address, but you better stay at different address, so then your spouse, children, parents and other family member does not get disturbed. It is just you that paid as CEO, not them. So let them free from disturbance, unneeded guest and criminal offences (kidnapping crimes, etc).

---

[109] Italian term used to refer to photojournalists who specialize in candid photography of celebrities, politicians, and other. http://www.mrpaparazzi.com

0081. 2nd Benefit: Less Worrying Tight Scary Schedules

Please make yourself easier to be understood by subordinates and business relation. Just make everything KISS (*kept it* as *short* and *simple*), and generating AIDA (*attention, interest, desires* to make proposed *actions*).[110]

What ever the lengths of speeches be given to you, always do it PREPARE (*point, reason, example,* and *point* to *audience, relations* and *enterprise*'s subordinates). After doing these, your tight schedules would be loosened.

You could use CARE (*capital, asset, revenue* and *earnings*) to identify CADREX (*capital, asset, debt, revenue, earnings* and *expenses*) to define 8 common financial ratios possible for all the company in this world:[111]

1)ROE= return on equity; 2)ROA= return on asset, 3)ATO= asset turnover, 4)NPM= net profit margin, 5)CAR= capital asset ratio, 6)DAR= debt asset ratio, 7)XER= expense ratio and 8)DER= debt equity ratio.

Tight schedules are only for dependent and difficult person that are not you. As a simpler and smarter free person, you better be a master, sitting on top of your schedule. It could be a very good servant, or a very cruel master to you!

---

[110] **KISS** is an acronym for the design principle "**Keep it simple, Stupid!**". http://en.wikipedia.org/wiki/KISS_principle

[111] Generic geometric finance terminologies possible for any IFRS or GAAP companies for extremely quick merger and acquisition finance. http://id.linkedin.com/pub/steve-asikin/35/5a9/765

0082. 3ⁿᵈ Benefit: Significant Productivity Improvement

Your subordinate will be very useful if work on firm chain of command duties[112] and concentric objectives. You might be very surprise that any industrious person, could not be useful to your organization if they do not follow hierarchy.

There are four types of subordinates according to the Diligence and Smartness. Surprisingly the very Smart an very Diligent persons are not the best assets for the organization, and the most Stupid and most Lazy person is not the worse member of the effective organization!

1)X-crossed (extinguish) personnel are they who are Diligent but Stupid, they use organizational resources unwisely and use more to impress leader and other member.

2)D (delegated) personnel are those who are very Diligent and very Smart. They are able and willing to do job that is Important but not Relevant to the Commander.

3) C (cammerad) person are those who are Stupid but Lazy. They are wrong but not using so many resources.

4)B (best brain) personnel are those who are very Smart but very Lazy. They will make all-things done quickly. Commander and head quarter need advices from this staffs.

---

[112] **Helmuth Karl Bernhard Graf von Moltke** (26 October 1800, Parchim, Mecklenburg-Schwerin – 24 April 1891) was a German Field Marshal. The chief of staff of the Prussian Army for thirty years, he is regarded as one of the great strategists of the latter 19th century, and the creator of a new, more modern method of directing armies in the field. He is often referred to as **Moltke the Elder** to distinguish him from his nephew Helmuth Johann Ludwig von Moltke, who commanded the German Army at the outbreak of World War I.
http://en.wikipedia.org/wiki/Helmuth_von_Moltke_the_Elder

0083. 4th Benefit: Better Priority Set for Future Cases

If the CEO plans the B (book later) schedule carefully, the organization will get much benefit from careful planning in a more efficient and creative way to perform wonderfully.

The word had been hypnotized by capitalist vs socialist continuum for long, and no one ever think differently.

Then a Chinese leader said that 1)Since the resources are limited and poverty is dangerous, they will use socialist style to manage resources and lowest poverty allowed. 2)But wealth and market opportunity is unlimited, so let capitalist go as high as possible in legal manner without pushing other. 3)The rest is history, now China is world's number two in economy and become its greatest in very near future.[113]

Not all the CEOs understand the financial statement (balance-sheet and income statement). They give that matters to accounting and they fail because accountant's interest is different than CEO's. It is a myth of financial difficulties.

What CEO must know is that balance sheet is moment picture of Asset, Capital and Debts, while income statement is a collective periodic Revenue, Expenses and Earnings. It takes only 4 items to do financial management and corporate health control: CARE (capital, assets, revenue and earnings).

---

[113] This page is about biography of **Deng** Xiaoping: "It doesn't matter whether the **cat** is black or **white**, as long as it catches mice. In 1931, he worked with Mao to establish the bases of the **Red** Army in the south-central province of Jiangxi.
http://www.library.thinkquest.org/26469/movers-and-shakers/deng.html

0084. 5th Benefit: Bringing More Confidence of Ability

What is relation between '*ability*' and '*confidence*'? It could be difficult, but those are two things learned and do supporting each other. If it runs for more than five years, both two grown well and the CEO be even stronger.

More '*ability*' brings '*confidence*', and '*confidence*' gets more '*ability*', etc. Those two will always growing if nothing bad stops them two. So try to have either one of them and starts growing, be stronger and stronger from time.

Two group of the same capable students given same test to assess the said capability. One group stated as '*capable*' group that all of the member said as pass the test. The other equal group stated as '*incapable*' group that all of the member said as could not pass the test.[114]

Although those two are not true the '*capable*' group becoming more '*capable*' and more '*confidence*' by the positive encouragement. The '*incapable*' group also becomes less capable and less confidence by negative encouragement.

This empirical evidence said that even '*confidence*' is a subjective feeling, while the '*capability*' is an objective state based on scientific test, those two proven as supporting each other. It is easy to understand that capable person feel more confidence than incapable person, but it is also proven that with the absence of confidence, learning process thought as more difficult and be very hard to increase the capability.

---

[114] One group stated as capable group that all of the member said as pass the test. http://www.easy-hub.org/stephan/kelly-its06.pdf

0085. 6th Benefit: Better Resources from Giant Within

The '*confidence*' and '*capability*' game test also be similar to the CEO as a person. If the CEO get praised by relevant party, then both '*confidence*', '*creativity*' and '*capability*' be better. Mostly the organization be better.

The main difference between student group test and CEO's is the organizational capability, mostly measured by the SWOT (*strengths, weaknesses, opportunities* and *threats*) which are more reality based than just subjective opinions.

On a certain degree '*confidence*', increase '*creativity*' and it later also increase the '*capability*' of the organization. It is not yet all, but it does help a lot. The inner potential is like a giant and could be awaken by proper impulse.

Let us count your blessing. Yes, name them one by one, then you see how lucky you are with the 96% to 99,2% time saving and you could only have a rush urgency on just 0.8% to 4% of total time possible, and it still going better![115]

Now, again please take your time to retreat and try to imagine how with just 4% individual action, you could and hopefully hath done 64% excellence. You could easily get 100% excellence by just do 6.25% individual actions there!

---

[115] "Lain **syakartum la adzi danakum** wala in kafartum inna adzabila sadid", **Count your Blessings** Name them **One by One**, **Count your blessings** see what GOD hath done! Always be Thankful for everything you have been blessed with in.
http://www.southernsoapopera.com/.../**count-your-blessingname-them-one**

CEO Time-Matrix

High Relevance

20%

	A
	0.8%

C = 16%   B = 3.2%

X = 64%   D = 16%

80%

Low Relevance

Low Importance
80%

High Importance
20%

B (book later) quadrant= 20% x 20% = 4% works
The remaining time = 100% - 64% - 16% -16% - 4% = 0%

B (book later) quadrant= 80% x 80% = 64% result
The remaining result = 100% - 4% - 16% -16% - 64% = 0%

0087. **CHAPTER-VI:**
      A (Act Now), or 0.8% as Core Essence Quadrant

After all, as the CEO you must still do things that are Relevant, Important but also Urgent. Not all the activities could be left undone. At least some of them must still done by the CEO themselves. They already very small in portion.

It is just 20% x 20% x 20% = 0.8% from CEO total time possibilities. This is the A (act now) quadrant. Please use this quadrant for doing the things that really Relevant, Important and Urgent for CEO strategic achievements.[116]

If the press and public want to hear something from the CEO, please do creative things that are very Interesting, Contrast to others, Positive, Memorable and very Logical to demonstrate the benefit of the organization to stake holders. It should be different and reversing compared to competitors.[117]

No one ever more attractive than the powerful CEO that makes a news. Press will follow the CEO that make nice logical statement that never been thought by commons.
Since common thing itself is not really common, press and public creative CEO that make sense and seems like has make fantastic logical improvement to common beliefs exist.

---

[116] Being committed to the social, economic and environmental health of communities we serve is as integral to our success as pleasing our guests. http://www.sites.**target**.com/site/en/corporate/page.jsp?contentId=PRD03

[117] To be successful today, a company must become **competitor oriented**. It must look for weak points in the positions of its competitors. http://www.dustyvolumes.com/archives/754

0088. All High Relevance, High Importance and Urgent

CEO must make the organization perceived as first. Number one is far more powerful than any better, bigger, cheaper, works harder, serve more, nicer, etc. Winner takes all, if your organization is not number one, so it is a follower.

What is the most spoken language in earth? English
Who is the first western leader landed in America? Columbus
What is the world's largest waterfall? Niagara
Who is the world's longest monarch now? Queen Elizabeth II
What is the world's longest dynasty ever? Japan (Yamato)

CEO must try to make their organization be number one, because the number one takes all and number two going nowhere. Public, press and common people had very limited memory so they could not remember who are the second.[118]

So why your organization be number three or less? It is painful and extremely hard to take from that position off. If it could not be number one, please make sure that at least can be a strong number two, with significant contrast to number one. Let conservative take number one and new generation takes the secured number two if those two are contrast.[119]

---

[118] **Winner-take-all** connotes also the principle of the Plurality voting system. This article is about the computational principle. **Winner-take-all** is a computational. http://www.en.wikipedia.org/wiki/**Winner-take-all**

[119] Respectively introduced in the year 1886 and 1903, both **Coca-Cola** and **Pepsi** were rivals each other trying to dominate the carbonated soft drink market. http://www.businessinsider.com/difference-**coke-pepsi**-people-2011

0089. After Removing 99.2% of Potential Time Waster

Please consider that all answer in the last page is perceived as true by many audiences. So being the number in customer's mind must be the main objective of CEO works. The CEO must use this A (act now) quadrant to be number one in stake holder's mind! Those not necessary the reality.

The last page is subjective as believed but no fact:
Earth's most spoken language is Mandarin, not English[120]
First western leader in America is Ericson, not Columbus[121]
World's largest waterfalls is the Iguazu, not Niagara[122]
Longest monarch now is King Bhumibol, not Elizabeth II[123]
Longest dynasty is Dulo (Bulgaria), not Japan (Yamato)[124]

---

[120] The 30 **most spoken languages** in the world: (1)Mandarin – Chinese Characters, (2) English – Latin. http://www.krysstal.com/**spoken**.html

[121] **Leif Ericson** a Norse explorer is regarded as the first European to in North America (excluding Greenland), 500 years before Columbus. http://www.en.wikipedia.org/wiki/**Leif_Ericson**

[122] **Iguazu Falls** is the top destinations in South America. Taller than Niagara Falls, the water level rises and falls with the season. http://www.gosouthamerica.about.com/cs/southamerica/a/**IguazuFalls**.htm

[123] The Queen surpassed George III on Thursday to become the second-**longest** reigning British **monarch** in more than 1000 years. http://www.en.wikipedia.org/.../Current_reigning_**monarchs**_by_length_of_reig

[124] The dynasty that ruled the longest in history is the Dulo Clan or the House of Dulo of Bulgaria. It ruled for 2,890 years. http://socyberty.com/history/10-dynasties-that-reigned-the-longest-in-history/

0090. Only 0.8% Remaining of 12500% Bigger Capacity

Exceptional CEO would work only at sensitive most activities those significant and strategic for the organization. Since all of the officers and subordinates work in their field, the CEO works to make the organization well accepted by targeted stake holders. Only CEO can do this.[125] The 0.8% work time opportunity must be effectively used for consciously planned activities. If the CEO could handle the organization well, he must try to push as many job from A (act now) quadrant to B (book later) quadrant.

At the next step, the CEO must also push as many as possible works from B (book later) quadrant to D delegate) and X-cross (extinguish) quadrant. The objective of this book is not to make CEO does not work at all, but to make the optimum most of the CEO working time possible. The world has some evidence that a CEO could make miracle in a very short time given, like the case of Iacoca,[126] Churchil,[127] and others. They make a contrarian significant short work against other, that brings very long strategic advantages.

---

[125] International surveys show that more than half of an **organization's reputation** can be attributed to the **CEO**. According to US research conducted. http://www.cuttingedgepr.com/articles/corprep_important.asp

[126] People have the capacity stand by nonchalantly witnessing a **miracle**, then walk. Attention has given to Lee **Iacocca's** sudden rise to fame. http://www.mirainternational.com/books/difference/chap12.htm

[127] We Shall Fight on the Beaches is a common title given to a **speech** delivered by Winston **Churchill** to the House of Commons of the Parliament of the United Kingdom. http://www.en.wikipedia.org/wiki/We_shall_fight_on_the_beaches

0091.   Utilize the 12400% Extra Time for More Impacts

One of the main jobs that CEO could not delegate to others is making impressive speeches that bring maximum benefit to the organization. As a leader the CEO must lead the troop and commanding the squad means speak well.[128]

The second thing that leader must do after speeches of establishing direction, is being the role model for the people to follow. In this sense the trusted, productive, consistent and smart CEOs make the organization better than who are not.

Please carefully think those, because the CEO must do them all in just 0.8% to 4% of the total time possible. The A (act now) and B (book later) quadrant must be managed very contrast and positive to gain organizational impacts.

The organization will fail if the CEO could not speak them a clear direction to go, or the leader does not behave as excellent role model in order to accomplish that. In this sense, it is very much logical that 4% CEO actions that very well managed consciously is better than 100% normal one!

---

[128] Leader's primary mission is to influence people, (a)Leaders are responsible for influencing others for changing how they think and feel so that, ultimately, they will change how they act. (b) Speaking is a leader's most effective tool of influence. At impromptu pep talk or a major presentation, leaders have the opportunity to influence listeners. (c)Speeches every leaders need present: "Who We Are", Articulates the organization's IDENTITY. "Why We Do What We Do", Promotes the organization's VALUES. "Where We Are Headed", Advances the organization's MISSION. http://www.wittcom.com/Three_Speeches.htm

0092. Additional Pareto's Advancement for Winners

Like common military leaders, the CEO must use a very short appearance of productive (effective and efficient) action to impress the whole organization to follow and work together in well segregated manner to achieve desired states.

After battle of Agincourt the British archers think for a long pre-strained crossbow, to improve both ordinary long distance difficult longbow-short distance efficient crossbows. So they could use 3.2% time in preparation and the rest 0.8% to aim on the right target. It does work better than ever.[129]

Back to the basic strategy, please be consistent to X-cross (extinguish) the 64% of time wasters because those are not Relevant and neither important to the organization. Also D (delegate) the 16 % that is Important for organization and not Relevant for CEO. This is very Important, so dangerous if done by CEO alone. Please let as many Able and Willing subordinates to work there and safe 16% CEO times.

The remaining 20% are things that are Relevant to the role of CEO, so those should be done diligently. Quadrant C (contingency) is 80% of them or 16% from total CEO time should be accurately file documented. At the end the B (book later) quadrant should be employed productively, so then the essential 0.8% could be used by CEO for greatest impacts.

---

[129] The Battle of **Agincourt** demonstrated the superior battlefield tactics of the ordinary military **crossbow** in range, rate of fire, and accuracy. http://www.amazon.ca/...Agincourt-Crossbow-Crossbows/dp/1157602886

0093. 1st Benefit: More Time for Additional Pleasures

Managing the CEO total time by (64% + 16%) +(16% +3.2% + 0.8%), is very much beneficial. The organization could achieve more of its Important target by most of the Able and Willing member, without too much stressing burden on CEO time usages. The responsibility is still with the CEO, but its operational works could be multiplied and better done.

Both organization and CEO could also eliminate things that are not Important, but sure it is a CEOP role to keep strong Relevant document filing and easy retrieve system for contingency purposes. So organization be safer.

After eliminated by (64% + 16%) Irrelevant job and 16% contingent safety preparation, the CEO could concentrate on 3.2% Tickler scheduling[130] for better delayed items and 0.8% of must done fantastically activities.[131]

This book is a 'how-to' tool. It is not talk much about theories, although it contains so many. Easy reader quickly gets its main message by a quick review on its Title, Table, Introduction and Head of pages. More diligent readers could read all quickly in less than an hour. Finally the party who are much more interested could read the footnotes & their webs.

---

[130] Many of these **systems** known as **document** imaging **systems**, because they focused on capture, storage, indexing and retrieval of image **file**. http://www.en.wikipedia.org/wiki/**Document**_management_system

[131] Only highest and purest thoughts will touch down within your mind and there will be only way to be one **truth** to **speak**. Take a **moment** to this. http://www.allegoricallyspeaking.blogspot.com/2011/08/**moment**-of-**truth**.html

0094. 2nd Benefit: Less Worrying Tight Scary Schedules

Schedules are set to be followed and done, not to be worried for. If the objective is clear, then the 64% X-cross (extinguish) quadrant must quickly dropped out. Then the 16% D (delegation) to the Able and Willing members could quickly assign for organizational important matters.

The most difficult thing and sometimes unclear is the C (contingency), because most of the CEOs do this as D (delegating) to the trusted subordinates. *First mistake*, this Relevant role is C (contingent) and very dangerous to be D (delegated). *Second mistake*, subordinate not really Able & Willing for doing this.That will place CEO in danger![132]

Sure the CEO might asked the secretary and office boys to do help, but they should be told (CEO do Telling). Most of them are Unable and Unwilling to do this Relevant CEO job. So then close CEO real time control is needed. Its most important function is to be retrieved quickly by CEO.

Succession and handover will raise legal issues to CEO responsibility. It is very much suggested ofr the predeceasing CEO to make an independent professional audit, as a strong legal evidence of the situation while leaving the company.

Restated statements could also be done by successor, to disgrace the successful predecessor, but strong legal audit from reputable independent party will defend predecessor.

---

[132] Many companies have, or soon will, replace their outgoing **CEOs**. Each of these cases has unique characteristics and associated **dangers.** http://www.psychologytoday.com/.../**executive**-succession-there-will-be

0095. 3nd Benefit: Significant Productivity Improvement

Please make at least a significantly better productivity while CEO still led the company. Without strong and bold evidence, the predecessor will suffer. It is common that any successor will state that predecessor are not really as good as what people believe while he or she was in the CEO position.

Making false statement less than actual performance, is not a tactic that is recommended by this book, but are commonly practiced by any successor. Please be prepared and be careful and never let yourself become a victim of this.

Significant productivity improvements will make the CEO looks great, but gaining public respect for long, much longer than the '*golden age*' itself really experienced.[133] So, let us be careful to make strong evidences, since all next rulers will always tempted to rewrite your achievement as less.

Please be smart on this. It is true that you just work as a today's CEO and you did it well as God almighty witnessing them. That is not yet the truth, since bad performances will easily forgotten and be improved but great performances are normally discounted to be seen as more common.[134] It is like faster growing grass in the field, will be cut for uniformity.

---

[133] In **history**, civilizations contributed to the cultural and intellectual life of humanity. These are often called **Golden Ages**, to them as society. http://www.regentsprep.org/Regents/global/themes/**goldenages**/index.cfm

0096. 4th Benefit: Better Priority Set for Future Cases

After you understand much of the CEO's (64% + 16%) + (16% + 4%) principle, then it is clearer that you are living by now on, but your good performance will still be discussed many-many years after. Welcome to eternity![135]

You better set your Vision and Mission clearly. What will you do extremely well and how later people will perceive you based on the future perceptions and standards? Will you are still looked as great? How could you improve it now? If it is still hard to make a good use of your 0.8% or 4% time, how could you control the quality of your 100% time? It is almost impossible. On the contrary if you could manage your 0.8% and 3.2% well, the rest be a legend!

The wise man said that time is precious and will never be set back. Now even the idiot knows that CEO time is even more precious and must be carefully managed. Not all of the people had chance to lead others as CEO, so use that well! Please again be consider that becoming a CEO is not a reward for your past performances. Rather it is a duty for achieving future opportunities, that its responsibility will be collected right after your significant decisions done.[136]

---

[134] The tendency is to score everyone around the midpoint of the scale, and not use the extremes. The result of this is the **central tendency error**.
http://www.jrank.org/business/pages/181/central-tendency-bias.html

[135] Ace Greenberg is the **Legendary CEO** of Bear Stearns. Greenberg is also the author of the best selling Memos from the Chairman.
http://www.streetstories.com/ag_fw_top100.html

[136] Military family knows that service person may be killed in duty, but may accept that risk because they understand the values of **duty** and **honor.** http://www.au.af.mil/au/awc/awcgate/au-24/au24-352mac.htm

0097. 5th Benefit: Bringing More Confidence of Ability

Please remind and still be considered that CEO is also a Commander for the organization. Most of the people join the organization to '_earn a living_" or as a '_bread winner_' for the family. They really need their organization to win.[137]

That purpose had become more sacred in this modern world, where the riches seeing this as a game of getting more luxuries by pushing some others far below the poverty line. CEO must all member's family had ample food and money.

A confidence CER must seriously do bold aligning acts to make sure that the entire organizational member had the correct opinion about the situations and the collective actions they do for making things better for their families.[138]

The CEO must eliminate the room for any individual subjective opinions, and let all the member see them alike to the problems, situations and solutions seem by organization.

If anybody does not agree to shared organizational vision, then both the organization and those individuals must make legal separation as quickly as possible, so then could not disturbing other loyal member in the chain of command.

---

[137] Moreover, a **breadwinner** had far more chances to fail than did the **success.** Although I have attributed the development of the "male **breadwinner** family". http://www.dearcupid.org/question/i-think-its-a-mans-**duty**-to-be.html

[138] A leader's efforts to develop a **shared vision** have been described as. To study their superintendents' vision included "deciding what's the **correct** thing to do. http://www.sedl.org/change/issues/issues23.html

0098. 6th Benefit: Better Resources from Giant Within

If the CEO is the seed, then the organization is the field to grow and multiply the good things brought by CEO. Pleasant climate for learning does help to make all members aiming for the same direction and let no one be poor.

During the limited 4% time the CEO must plan to make all of them be possible. It's 3.2% for consciously plan it on CEO's Relevant and Important Role and 0.8% to actually done by the CEO to gain the greatest organizational benefit.

If seen from the CEO sight, the case is 0.8% A (act now), 3.2% B (book later), 16% C (contingent), 16% D (delegated) and 64% X-cross (extinguish) actions. It works consecutively based on priority scale and SWOT analysis. [139]

Ancient eastern leadership said that their leader is the one that could block '*hidden arrows*' and '*unseen bad evils*' that disturb their organization to achieve the common goal. Life is hard. Being a family bread winner is even harder. So the CEO position is purely sacred with heavy responsibility in the eye of God almighty and human being as well. Are you ready?!! Let us walk in the red carpet of the elders, now! [140]

---

[139] The very first suggestion, from a user called *Tzimisces*, also proved to be clear favourite among other readers: Carl Philipp Gottlieb von **Clausewitz.** http://www.economist.com/blogs/**clausewitz**

[140] **Ancient Eastern Philosophy** is rich in wisdom & beauty. Understood the dynamic unity of reality, interconnection of all things and harmonious moral. http://www.en.wikipedia.org/wiki/**Eastern_philosophy**

CEO Time-Matrix

**High
Relevance**

A

20%

	0.8%
C = 16%	B = 3.2%
X = 64%	D = 16%

80%

**Low
Relevance**

**Low Importance
80%**

**High Importance
20%**

A (act now) quadrant= 20% x 20% x 20% = 0.8% works
The remaining time = 100% - 64% - 16% -16% - 4% = 0%

B (book later) quadrant= 80% x 80% x 80% = 51.2% result
Remaining result = 100% - 4% - 16% -16% - 3.2% = 0.8%

0100. CLOSING REMARK:
The Time Priority and Life Mathematics

THE SACRED TARGET

Never	Be Done
Proposeed	Not Done
Better	Avoided
Not	Regulated
Proposed	Done
Must	Done
1	*Wajib*
2	*Sunna*
3a	*Muba*
3b	*Subhat*
4a	
4b	*Makruh*
5	*Haram*

0101. Life is a Place of Worship

At least you have yourself exist in this world. You could feel and also seen your own, and you do have power. Since you also suppose to know your SWOT (strengths, weaknesses, opportunities and threats), you must maintain your strengths to get opportunities and avoiding threats on weaknesses. You must maintain and respect (worship) them!

From previous pages you know that there are 5 to 7 categories those must be treated differently:

1. Must be done (*wajib*)
2. Better be done (*suna*)
3. Not regulated (*muba*)
4. Better not be done (*makruh*)
5. Never be done, strictly prohibited (*haram*)

There is also doubtful are between the number 3 and number 4 (*subhat*), classified as point 3b and 4a.[141]

This respectful maintenance (worship) will also be more difficult if you depend on greater power outside yourself: Boss, Commander, Protecting Spirit, Demon, god, or God almighty that majority of world's people believe at.

Your worship will be more complicated, but you feel better. It is not important on whom that you truly believe, but how much the worshiping ritual could make you better.

---

[141] It is wrong to assume that people of other faiths do not understand the benefits of **Islamic laws** and that they will come once they have seen. http://www.bbc.co.uk/religion/religions/**islam**/beliefs/sharia_1.shtml

0102. Life is a Place of Wealth

The set of knowledge to make limited resources fairly distributed is called as economics. As proven in the history, the socialist approach performs better in poverty eradication and capitalist school of thought works better to make people achieving the highest standard of excellence possible.[142]

It is mandatory for any authority to make none of its people living below the poverty line, and it is not important to limit the riches, if they do not push other to live below the bottom limit (poverty line). Minimum influence is better.

Second, the authority must implement strong and non discriminative law to limit crime exist of taking some others' proprietary in unfair manner. Armed forces and all social activities must be governed by law. Unlawful is prohibited!

Since people will make wrong decision if not given clear information, so the authority must let their rights and responsibilities are clear and ample opportunities given to one that are better or willing to work fairly in achieving more.

Meritocracy is the best thing to move on social ladder while political alliances just benevolence for the allies and not always good for others. Democracy is nice in the concept but in most cases, the few statesmen manipulate the less smart voters. Corporate CEO is easier, because democracy runs among the company owners and not by unowned voters.

---

[142] The word economy can be traced back to the Greek word **oikonomos**, from **oikonomos** was derived oikonomi, which had not only the sense. http://www.thefreedictionary.com/economy

0103. Life is a Place of Warfare

After Second World War, all country borders had set and any changes are subject to the international acceptance. No one could be the country ruler if does not approved there.

Border trespassing at physical state could easily be verified and given back to its legal authority by international court's decision. So physical wealth is better guarded widely. Not so much war exists because of defending physical wealth.

Thing are more difficult in defending the spiritual or worshiping activities, because many conflicting values there. Slaying a black goat for ritual purposes might disturb other people's feeling that it is not proper if done outside abattoir.

Latin adagium said that who does want peace must be very much ready for war.[143] The world will be fairly regulated if the good party is in better power than the bad.

It seems good so far, but smart bad person might also take other's people rights, if the case is still doubtful and no strict rules prohibit that to be done in such manner.[144] To err and imperfect are human, ruler could improve it periodically after finding yet unregulated cases to be set for better future.

---

[143] **Si vis pacem, para bellum** is a Latin adage translated as, "If you wish for peace, prepare for war" (usually interpreted as meaning peace through strength). http://www.classicalvalues.com/archives/000013.html

[144] **Mullum delictum nulla poena sine praevia lege punali"**, was not actually an isolated legal principle. There are some legal principles prior. http://www.en.wikipedia.org/.../**Nullum_crimen,_nulla_poena_sine_prae via_lege**

0104. Satanic Finance & Time Management

Whether we like it or not, the current financial system in the world had been far away from justice. Hope these 3 cases in Satanic Finance make you better manage the time.

1)*Fiat money*: In non gold back-up, the US could buy a goat at US$ 100, which just cost them 4 cents = 0.04$ at US Burreau of Engraving. If the US really expensing 100 US$ worth, then they could get 2500 goats for it. So the country that sells goat will directly be poorer if US$ value go down. The US can safe time for not waiting the young goat goes old.

2)*Fractional reserve requirement*: With interbank checking account and clearing, a US bank could make more loans than the money it really has. On 100 US$ cash and 10% reserve requirement, the bank will receive the US$100 cash as customer deposit, and making US$ 90 loan which if then reinvested, could make another US$ 81 loan,[145] etc. These end with US$ 100 bank deposit at Federal Reserve and US$ 900 loans at US$ 1,000 customer deposit, from real US$ 100. Now the common bank had also creating checking moneys.

3)*Financial interest*: by giving US$ 900 loan the bank will book let us say 10% interest, so it means US$ 90 additional created money to the economy, that could make all prices goes up, starting from US$ 100 starting deposit. It makes US$ 1,000 bank asset add by US$ 90 newly booked. This demonstrates the effective time management in banking.

---

[145] How "money" is created in a fractional reserve banking system. M0 and M1 definitions of the money suppy. The multiplier effect. http://www.investopedia.com › Dictionary

0105.   The Aiming for Success Trap

It is unbelievable that there are so many people think that success is a destination; neither sees it as a journey. They set difficult and challenging goals and try working to realize them. They seldom successful and they feel very sad and fail.

They forget that success itself is just a bridge to feel happiness. Successful person is more likely to feel happy. What they do not consider is that happiness is just a feeling and people could feel happy even though they achieve none.

If they seriously decide to feel happy and now start affirming their blessings as evidences of their successes, the happiness will easily become theirs and they'll be success.

Back to this time management book, it is definitely Important and Relevant to make the organization feel success in the very beginning and start collecting their evidences.[146]

So why are you waiting so long? Let us use the 0.8% time for establishing ease and listen actively. Make them work hard on the segregated duties productively, but keep yourself be a peaceful and relax CEO in your few time.[147]

---

[146] **Good leaders** practice ways to communicate their visions, tying future pictures to **reality.** People admire the heroism of those who can **suffer** without losing their trust in. http://www.basic-life-skills-made-easy.com/**good-leadership**-skills.html

[147] **Good leaders** balance their lives and well as their business. The fact is, if you have any imbalance in your life, your business world will **suffer.** http://www.prosperitymastercode.com/?p=617

0106. The Multi Tasking Trap

Why the CEO life does is difficult? Because they are very busy and hard to manage their time schedule, they have plenty of task must be done in short and bring them stress. If things just happen like that, then CEO had forgotten to manage the Able and Willing subordinates do the delegation. Rather than using just 0.8% to 4% of the total, CEO mostly used 50% to 100% time budget by self working very hard.

That is bad, because if the leader does not focus on the main job, then the secretary or other lower staff will start asking question to CEO as polite cover of order and direction.

Guidance and direction from lower level person that had less skills, experience and resources will quickly make the organization trapped in trouble. It is natural.

Absence of CEO control[148] over the most sensitive 0.8% to 4% of the CEO time could make CEO fixing many things at the same time. It seems as multi tasking, but it just really an urgent activities of the bad CEO time management.

This book is not hating the multi tasking CEO. Some condition might need that, but not on the very early time. Be comfortable first with the time management before does that!

---

[148] **veni**, **vidi**, **vici**. Real Term: Julius Caeser said this when discribed how/what he did on his campaign. (veni (I came), vidi (I saw), vici (I conquered). Good time management! http://www.en.wikipedia.org/wiki/**Veni,_vidi,_vici**

0107.   The Core Essence of Happiness

One of the objective of this 'how-to' for CEO time management book is to make you glad and be happier from time to time, starting now up to the eternity. Please be glad that you are the CEO appointed for this sacred duty. Please go to your source of power that has proven you providing best power as needed, be always tight up to that.

Please carefully select the 64% X-cross (extinguish0, then 16% D (delegate), so then you only do 20% things that are Relevant to CEO job. Now you are in proper job box.

Please put the 16% Relevant but less Important as C (contingent), and protect yourself by an easy retrievable strong document system filing. Let this box work as proper.

Now please concentrate to the 4% that is Important and relevant, do tickler on 3.2% B (book later) activities and make a regular review on its Importance and Relevance.

Finally, please make a good use of your 0.8% A (act now) premium time to gain as much organizational benefit as possible and let all stake holders following your leadership.

Last, but not least: Please decide to classify yourself as a happy person and start collecting success time to time.[149]

---

[149] **Carpe diem** is a phrase from a Latin poem by Horace (see "Source" section below) that has become an aphorism. It is popularly translated as "seize the day".
    http://www.quotegarden.com/**carpe-diem**.html

0108. **REFERENCES**

AMIN, Riawan. *Indonesia Militan*, Celestial Publishing, Jakarta, 2009

AMIN, Riawan. *Satanic Finance*, Senayan Abadi Publishing, Jakarta, 2008

AMIN, Riawan. *The Celestial Management*, Amazon.com, Seattle, 2011

AMIN, Riawan. *You are (not) the Boss*, Celestial Publishing, Jakarta, 2010